W9-APH-032

# PRINCIPAL
# MENTORING

## A **Safe, Simple,** and **Supportive** Approach

## Carl J. Weingartner

Foreword by John C. Daresh

A Joint Publication

**CORWIN PRESS**
A SAGE Company

*For information:*

Corwin Press
A SAGE Company
2455 Teller Road
Thousand Oaks, California 91320
www.corwinpress.com

SAGE Ltd.
1 Oliver's Yard
55 City Road
London EC1Y 1SP
United Kingdom

SAGE Pvt. Ltd.
B 1/I 1 Mohan Cooperative
    Industrial Area
Mathura Road, New Delhi 110 044
India

SAGE Asia-Pacific Pte. Ltd.
33 Pekin Street #02-01
Far East Square
Singapore 048763

Printed in the United States of America

*Library of Congress Cataloging-in-Publication Data*

Weingartner, Carl J.
Principal mentoring: a safe, simple, and supportive approach/Carl J. Weingartner. A joint publication with the National Staff Development Council.
        p. cm.
Includes bibliographical references and index.
ISBN 978–1–4129–6596–5 (cloth)
ISBN 978–1–4129–6597–2 (pbk.)

    1. First-year school principals—In-service training—United States. 2. Mentoring in education—United States. I. Title.

LB2831.92.W438 2009
371.2′012—dc22                                    2008024370

This book is printed on acid-free paper.

08   09   10   11   12   10   9   8   7   6   5   4   3   2   1

| | |
|---|---|
| *Acquisitions Editor:* | Arnis Burvikovs |
| *Associate Editor:* | Desirée A. Bartlett |
| *Production Editor:* | Veronica Stapleton |
| *Copy Editor:* | Alison Hope |
| *Typesetter:* | C&M Digitals (P) Ltd. |
| *Proofreader:* | Dennis W. Webb |
| *Indexer:* | Sheila Bodell |
| *Cover Designer:* | Karine Hovsepian |

# Contents

Foreword                                                    ix
    *John C. Daresh*

Preface                                                     xiii

Acknowledgments                                             xvii

About the Author                                            xxi

Introduction                                                1

1. Advocating for the Beginning Principal                   3
    Why Mentoring in Our District?                          3
    The Anatomy of a Beginning Principal                    5
    Professional Organizations                              6
    Scenario: Sharing the Wealth                            7
    Key Points                                              8
    Recommended Reading                                     8

2. The Beginning of a Mentor Program                        9
    APS District Demographics                               9
    The Birth of the Albuquerque Mentor Program             10
    Budget Justification                                    10
    Selecting a Coordinator                                 12
    Key Points                                              13
    Recommended Readings                                    13

3. A Work in Process                                        15
    The First Stages of Development                         15
    Vision and Mission Statements                           16
    Program Guidelines                                      17
    Job Descriptions                                        18
    Program Process                                         20
    A Total Support System for New Principals               21
    Key Points                                              23
    Recommended Readings                                    23

4. Program Implementation 25
 Step 1. The Process Begins 25
 Step 2. The Initial Coordinator-Mentee Meeting 26
 Step 3. Conferring With the Mentor 27
 Step 4. The Planning Session 29
 Step 5. The Other 5 Percent 29
 Key Points 32
 Recommended Readings 32

5. Simple Program Enhancements Make a Difference 33
 Congratulate 33
 Celebrate 33
 Communicate 34
 Appreciate 35
 The Morale Factor 36
 Scenarios: Extra Support for Supporters 36
 Key Points 38
 Recommended Readings 38

6. Applying the Mentoring Concept to Small School Districts 39
 Organize a Study Committee 41
 Purpose of the Study Committee 41
 Scenario: A Simple Form of Mentoring 45
 Key Points 47
 Recommended Reading 48

7. The Accountability Factor 49
 End-of-the-Year Evaluations 49
 Alternative Assessments 49
 Program Evaluations 54
 ESP Ten-Year Program Assessment (1995–2005) 56
 Key Points 59
 Recommended Readings 59

8. The Art of Mentoring the Beginning Principal 61
 Concepts for Effective Mentoring 62
 Establishing the Mentor Pool 63
 Suggestions for Mentors Working With Mentees 66
 Mentoring Versus Coaching 68
 A Coaching Concept 69
 Simplicity 70
 Level-to-Level Mentoring 71
 Communicate, Communicate, Communicate 71
 Scenario: A Mentor's Wisdom 72

Key Points                                                             74
Recommended Readings                                                   74

9.  Finding Time to Become an Instructional Leader                     75
    It's a Matter of Time                                              76
    Time-Management Suggestions                                        76
    The Importance of Strong Instructional Leadership                  78
    Demographic Data for Instructional Implementation                 79
    The Evaluation Process                                             81
    Scenario: Reciprocal Mentoring                                     81
    Key Points                                                         83
    Recommended Readings                                               83

10.  Caution, Pitfalls Ahead!                                          85
     It's About Time                                                   85
     The Funding Dilemma                                               86
     Plan, Plan, Plan                                                  86
     Do Not Take Stress and Burnout Lightly                           87
     Scenario: A Heavy Load                                            89
     Superintendents and Upper-Level Administration                   92
     Scenario: Solve the Problem                                      92
     Key Points                                                        93
     Recommended Readings                                              95

11.  Reflections                                                       97
     Recommended Readings                                              99

References                                                            101

Index                                                                 103

# Foreword

Educational research in the early 1980s that looked into the issue of what factors contribute to effective schools discovered a fact that many educators had known for many years: Effective schools have effective leaders serving as their principals. A completely new movement was launched by those who suddenly rediscovered that the person "down the hall from the classrooms" was an important person, particularly if he or she devoted most or all of his or her time to supporting good practice by teachers. "Instructional leadership" became the key to all the good that was to happen in schools everywhere, and principals were rediscovered.

A few years after this rediscovery, however, another reality began to appear in schools across the United States. Principals—important ingredients of successful schools—were beginning to retire at an amazingly high rate. Individuals who joined the ranks of teachers in the 1950s and 1960s were leaving schools and leaving the duties of serving as effective leaders to a whole new generation of people who would now move into the offices "just down the hall." The arrival of new and inexperienced principals became common in schools and districts across the nation.

But in addition to the need for new principals over the past two decades, new expectations for schools were becoming evident. The need to find schools that are more effective became the center of much of the daily dialogue of the political process across the country. Pressures to ensure that all schools would be successful and ensure that "no child" would be "left behind" have become realities to those who take on the challenges of leadership. Not only was there a great need for many new principals, but the new principals faced pressures and stress never experienced by their predecessors. Being a new principal is now more than simply learning how to do a managerial job: it is a daunting challenge to become a principal in a difficult environment.

Fortunately, the dilemma posed by needing new good principals who are able to perform effectively in a professional environment that is increasingly stressful has been recognized as an issue that needs attention. State departments of education, professional associations for school administrators, and individual school systems have launched numerous efforts to provide support and guidance to novice principals, with the assumption that such formal activities will help beginning principals survive their newly selected career paths in education. However, many of these efforts have been short lived, often because they were designed primarily to simply *appear* supportive of new principals, or because they were very costly to implement, or perhaps most inappropriately, because they became programs with a focus on *evaluating* and not necessarily *helping* principals.

By contrast, one program designed to assist newly appointed principals not only survive their first years, but also to thrive as instructional leaders, has been operating without a great deal of visibility or fanfare for more than a decade. It began with a simple observation by a retired principal who devoted the majority of his career in education as a dedicated leader and who never lost his enthusiasm for and love of the principalship. Carl Weingartner, author of this book, frequently witnessed the difficulties of his colleagues as they first stepped in to the principal's office. He believed that having more experienced principals around to answer questions, to serve as cheerleaders, and to anticipate and interpret political potholes would be a way to make the principalship more doable, with leaders who could devote more of their time to increasing the learning opportunities for students in their schools.

That was the beginning of the Extra Support for Principals (ESP) mentoring program, a truly exemplary model of how a single urban school district—the Albuquerque Public Schools, in New Mexico—has been able to keep the focus on the importance of helping principals achieve success in performing what daily becomes a more complex and stressful job. The underlying assumption of this effort that has guided the ESP mentoring program for more than a dozen years has been the motto, "Keep it safe, simple, and supportive." I believe the Albuquerque model has been able to survive because it has avoided the traps that other efforts have fallen into in creating programs to help new principals. It is not terribly costly, the operation of the program is not tied to pages filled with regulations and policies, and, above all, it holds true to one simple principle: experienced principals are the best source for providing true and meaningful support to new principals.

This book will provide you with detail about the design of a mentoring program that has served the needs of beginning principals in a large school system for several years. I believe that what Carl Weingartner describes can readily be adapted to support principals in very small districts, mid-size suburban districts, and even megadistricts. As a testimonial to that belief, I have been privileged to work with Carl and serve as a member of a consulting team that has been engaged in trying to fine-tune a program of mentoring and coaching for new principals in the Chicago Public Schools, the third-largest school district in the United States, for the past three years.

Safety, simplicity, and security remain the key ingredients of any mentoring program. Above all, though, as you read this work you will also quickly understand what additional "magic" ingredients must be present. Respect for colleagues and love of the principalship gave rise to Carl's work in developing the mentoring program; these same values will guide you in working through the suggestions offered to guide your efforts.

Principals are important people, and their job becomes more difficult each year. We are blessed to have resources such as this book and its author to make the job a more effective and satisfying place for great educators. I wish you success in your safe, simple, and secure efforts to create an environment that will help principals help children.

John C. Daresh, PhD

Professor of Educational Leadership

University of Texas of El Paso

Author and Consultant

# Preface

The principalship has become more challenging over the past ten years. Many school districts have looked at support systems such as mentoring and coaching to assist neophytes through their first year as principal. Best practices and research have been reviewed, and successful mentor programs have been developed across the nation that address growing concerns about principal recruitment and turnover. "After five years in the district, one-third of all principals hired had left that district," Dr. Susan Villani (2006, p. 9) cites the Denver Board of Education. Other districts across the nation can relate to similar statistics. Again as cited by Villani, the Institute for Educational Leadership identifies research that supports the theory that the principalship is in crisis, as does the National Association of Elementary School Principals (2001). Districts must make a concerted effort to address principal attrition by developing a process that encourages and supports experienced educators in pursuit of principal positions. Mentoring can be a significant segment of the total package needed to recruit, support, and retain effective principals.

In Albuquerque, this process began with a small group of principals reflecting on their first year as new principals. They recognized that their cohorts were the only means of support available in a nonthreatening atmosphere. This was their motivation for pursuing a formalized support system for new principal appointees. This group evolved into the Extra Support for Principals (ESP) advisory board.

The advisory board realized that a beginning principal comes into a new school setting having to adapt to all the responsibilities the predecessor may have handled with ease. New principals are aware that a district will have expectations that may include a variety of concerns, such as improving curriculum and test scores, student safety, or enhancing school climate. There may be a need to provide extra support in the areas of budget, instruction, state standards, or evaluation procedures for the newly appointed administrator. The Kentucky Association of School Administrations and the Appalachian Education Laboratory identified time management as the single most requested in-service topic by new principals (Villani, 2006, p. 7). Poor time management can become a contributing factor that can impact the health, mental state, and success and progress of the new administrator. Stress can lead to issues that may contribute to principal attrition rates. The Albuquerque Public Schools (APS) ESP advisory board embarked on a quest to provide a mentor program for new principals that would provide a **safe** environment, a **simple** format, and a professional **support** plan to minimize the feeling of isolation that new principals can experience. In the total support concept, I address district concerns while providing unencumbered mentoring for the new administrator as illustrated with the Venn diagram in Chapter 3. The "safe, simple, and supportive" concept evolved out of those concerns. This approach for extra support gives the mentor an opportunity to assist the new principal with growth and development as the mentee becomes an effective leader. It also provides opportunities to support and advise on district mandates, management, or operational issues. I address stress and burnout in Chapter 10.

As coordinator for a principal mentoring program in APS for the past twelve years, I have had the opportunity to share and exchange ideas with school districts, individual principals, doctoral students, researchers, consultants, and university professors across the nation. Although there are many successful mentor programs, increasing numbers of these programs have a brief lifespan of no more than three to five years. Why are these programs vulnerable? And, conversely, why has the program in APS lasted twelve years? Patterns emerge that have negative or positive impacts on programs. Certain established practices become predictors of success or failure of a program. I review these predictors at the end of Chapter 10.

*Principal Mentoring: A Safe, Simple, and Supportive Approach* will present successes and concerns of mentor program development. Mentoring is addressed on a supportive and comprehensive level. Additional mentoring approaches are recommended throughout the book. A significant concept of this book is the focus on the relationship between the mentee and the mentor. Mentees are often reminded that the objective of the program is not to create extra work and hardship, but rather to create an environment in which the new principal is safe and supported through a simple process. The book will be devoted to establishing and developing that safe, simple, and supportive approach. Chapters 3 and 4 will focus on the development and implementation of mentoring relationships. Chapter 10 focuses on some practices that might have a negative impact on the successes of a mentor program, and Chapter 11 encourages reflections on principal recruitment and retention.

Again, the purpose of this book is to share information about a successful mentor-mentee model and to provide insight that will stimulate innovative ideas and creative thinking within and among school districts, large or small, rural or isolated. My primary goal is to emphasize "how to," rather than "research shows."

---

### W.O.W.

Words of Wisdom will be injected on occasion into this document based upon the personal experiences of the author from the inception of his involvement with mentoring programs over the past 12 years.

---

*Source:* Dr. Jo Nelle Miranda, Retired Principal, University of New Mexico, Administration Intern Preparation Program.

# Acknowledgments

**M**any individuals have contributed to the success of the Albuquerque principals' mentor program. I want to acknowledge specific individuals at five levels of involvement and support.

First, I must acknowledge my wonderful family who supported and provided inspiration. To My Love—My Wife—Mary Lou Weingartner (August 3, 1941–October 31, 1993), whom I lost too early in life; to my wonderful daughters Erica, Amy, and Karin; to Karin's husband Eric Case and their sons Samuel and Thomas; and to my extended family Joanna Cramer, her daughter, her son-in-law, and her granddaughter (Denise, Brian, and Sadie Bickel), and Joanna's son Andrew Cramer. Thank you.

Second, thank you to the many Albuquerque principals who supported the mentor program for more than twelve years. I must recognize Peter Espinosa, Principal, Kirtland Elementary School, Albuquerque Public Schools (APS), and the Extra Support for Principals (ESP) advisory board for their dedication to the program. It was Peter's vision to pursue a mentor program. He was willing to invest time to organize a steering committee, which later became the advisory board. Peter served as chairperson of the board for twelve years. My gratitude to the board, which includes Bob Hennig, retired secondary principal; Russell Goff, retired secondary principal; Jim Steinhubel, secondary principal; Wayne Knight, secondary principal; Linda Sink, secondary principal; Dr. JoAnn Krueger, retired secondary principal and retired professor from the University of New Mexico; Dr. John Mondragon, retired APS regional superintendent, Central New Mexico Community College board member, and professor emeritus at the University of New Mexico; Eva Vigil, elementary principal; Marcella Jones, elementary principal; Victor Suazo, retired elementary principal; Ron Williams and John Miera, control agents; and Patricia Gilberto, retired elementary principal and executive director of the APS Principals Association. Although Dr. Krueger and Dr. Mondragon served as professors at the University of New Mexico, there was no official affiliation between the University of New Mexico and the ESP mentor program. The mentor program was an APS district initiative. This advisory board represented the heart of the mentor program; their guidance and knowledge were greatly appreciated.

The third level of involvement and support must include our district-level administrators. Without their willingness to support both the concept and the program, the program would not have survived. ESP is fortunate to have superintendents who can interject ideas while respecting the intent of the program. By working together, we have been able to develop a comprehensive program that met district needs while providing an individual support system for beginning principals. I am proud to acknowledge the support of the team of Dr. Elizabeth Everitt, superintendent; Susie Peck, associate superintendent; Nelinda Venegas, associate superintendent; Diego Gallegos, assistant superintendent; Andrea Trybus, executive director of human resources; and Amelia Gandara, project manager. The working relationship between district-level administrators and school principals has been one of discussion, compromise, and support.

The fourth level of acknowledgement includes appreciation for those who support the mentor program. They believe that the concepts provided in ESP are important. These include the APS staff and business sponsors who have graciously assisted the program over the years. I must acknowledge the special support from APS human resource secretarial staff members Cippie Chavez, Jo Anne Galindo, and Mary Lou Benevegna, as well as that of the APS superintendents' secretarial staff: Carol Vigil, Anna Armijo, Rita Roybal, and Tena Chavez.

Limited funding could eliminate many program amenities were it not for the business partners. Because of the support and generosity of Sharla Reinhart and Hena Torres of the New Mexico Educators Federal Credit Union; The Flower Company Staff; LaDonna Carley and Bob Skoglund of Portraits by LaDonna; and Karin Tarter, Lisa Lawrence, Michael Hazen, Judy Elder (retired), and the APS graphics production and district services staff, the mentor program has been enriched beyond budget limitations. Chapter 5 describes how the program utilized the generosity of our business partners and how their support enhanced the program. Business partners supported the principals' mentor program for most of the twelve years of the program's existence.

The fifth level includes the contributions of several experts in the field of the principalship. The knowledge and insight gained from their experience are invaluable to the mentor program as support is provided for neophyte administrators. For sharing their knowledge and expertise, I must acknowledge Dr. Jo Nelle Miranda, retired principal and editor; Dr. John Daresh, University of Texas at El Paso, professor, consultant, author, and lecturer; Dr. Lois Zachary, president of Leadership Development

Services, Phoenix, Arizona, consultant, author, and lecturer; Dr. Bruce Barnett, University of Texas at San Antonio, professor, consultant, author, and lecturer; Dr. Susan Villani, Senior Program and Research Associate at Learning Innovations at WestEd, Woburn, MA, consultant, author, and lecturer; and Gail Ward, Mary Beth Cunat, Linda Shay, Michael Alexander, Dr. Addie Belin-Williamson, and Dr. Dick Best from the Office of Principal Preparation and Development, Chicago Public Schools.

## PUBLISHER'S ACKNOWLEDGMENTS

Corwin Press gratefully acknowledges the contributions of the following individuals:

George W. Bayles
Principal
Timpview High School
Provo, UT

David Freitas
Professor
Indiana University South Bend
School of Education
South Bend, IN

C. Bruce Haddix
Principal
Center Grove Elementary School
Greenwood, IN

Alice Hom
Principal
NYC Department of Education
Public School 124
New York, NY

Jim Hoogheem
Retired Elementary School
   Principal
Maple Grove, MN

Deborah Long
Beginning Teacher Support and
   Assessment Induction
   Coordinator
Merced Union High School
Merced, CA

Andrew Nixon
Assistant Professor
University of West Georgia
Carrollton, GA

Stephen D. Shepperd
Principal
Sunnyside Elementary School
Kellogg, ID

# About the Author

**Carl J. Weingartner** has been an educator for more than forty-six years. He earned his bachelor's and master's degrees from East Central State University at Ada, Oklahoma, and completed postgraduate work in school administration at the University of New Mexico. He taught eleven years at the junior high and elementary levels in Gallup-McKinley County School District, Gallup, New Mexico; Midwest City and Del City School District, Midwest City, Oklahoma; and at the Albuquerque Public Schools District (APS), Albuquerque, New Mexico. He served as a junior high and elementary principal for twenty-two years in the APS District. He considers himself a practitioner rather than a researcher. After the death of his wife in 1993, he retired with thirty-three years of educational service.

In 1994, he was contracted by the Albuquerque Public Schools on a part-time basis to establish and coordinate the ESP mentor program for first-year principals. The program has involved and supported more than 210 first-year principals. He has become active in promoting mentor programs across the nation by writing and contributing to several organizational websites. He has written or contributed to articles and books for the National Association of Elementary School Principals, the National School Boards Association, the George Lucas Educational Foundation, and to the works of independent authors, including Dr. Susan Villani, author of *Mentoring and Induction Programs That Support New Principals* (Corwin Press, 2006). He has been asked to advise or consult with more than sixty-five individuals or institutions across the United States, Canada, and the United Kingdom. His assistance has helped several school districts establish principal mentor programs. He has given presentations on mentoring at the National Association of Elementary School Principals Conference in San Diego, California, and at the Arizona Department of Education Annual Conference in Phoenix, Arizona. Mr. Weingartner worked as a consultant for the "Transition to Teaching" teacher mentor program for two years. This program served the small rural school districts of Springer, Clayton, Cimarron, Raton, and Mosquero, New Mexico. He presently is instructing aspiring principals at New Mexico Highlands University Satellite, Rio Rancho, New Mexico, and is consulting for the Chicago Public Schools District, Office of Principal Preparation and Development/Effective Leaders Improve Schools Principal Mentor Project.

He has been active during his professional career in promoting education and the principalship. He served as president of several educational organizations including the National Association of Elementary School Principals, SCA-Zone VIII, the New Mexico Association of Elementary School Principals, and the APS Principals Association. He held several offices and served on executive boards and principal committees at the national, zone, state, and district levels. Weingartner has been a member of National Association of Elementary School Principals throughout his career as a principal and has maintained his membership since his retirement in 1994.

He has received honors and recognitions, including the National Distinguished Principal Award from the U.S. Department of Education in 1987. He has received Outstanding School Administrator Awards from the National Association of Elementary School Principals, the National Association of Elementary School Principals-Zone VIII, the New Mexico Association of Elementary School Principals, and the New Mexico School Administrators Association. "Carl J. Weingartner Day" was declared on March 20, 1981, in the City of Albuquerque by Mayor David Rusk. New Mexico Governors Bruce King, Jerry Apodaca, and Garry Carruthers also have recognized him for educational achievements. He received recognition in the United States Congressional Record and from the New Mexico State Board of Education and the APS Board of Education. Weingartner also received Outstanding Community Service Awards from the Boy Scouts of America, the Girl Scouts of America, Campfire Boys and Girls, and the Albuquerque Public Schools. Recently, he was inducted into his high school hall of fame at Varnum High School, Seminole, Oklahoma.

# Introduction

Extra Support for Principals (ESP) is a mentor program created in 1995 to provide support for beginning principals in the Albuquerque (New Mexico) Public Schools. From this program evolved the concept of providing a safe, simple, and supportive approach to mentoring principals. This book is about an approach to mentoring that is designed to provide support, develop leadership, and help alleviate stress for new principals as they transition into their new positions.

As mentor programs develop, they may tend to include other district concerns and initiatives; programs can be laden with other agendas that can overwhelm the neophyte administrator. The Albuquerque principals mentor program has made a conscious effort to avoid a pattern that creates stress rather than encourages growth.

Addressing the issues of principal shortages and attrition were major justifications for developing the program, with an emphasis on respecting time as it relates to both the responsibilities of the mentor and mentee. Stress can be alleviated to some degree with the support of a formal peer relationship. Discussing problems, concerns, and mandates with an experienced colleague can be comforting and reassuring to a new administrator who may feel somewhat isolated. It is the intent of the program to provide mentor support for the new principal without the mentor or mentee sacrificing their individual school responsibilities.

The ESP program continues to have one primary purpose: to provide an unencumbered support system for beginning principals. It is a program designed with a practical "how to" approach rather than a "research shows" process. Although research and best practices were utilized in the design of the program, the ultimate objective was based on the experiences and needs as conveyed by principals dealing with school issues. It is a voluntary program. Participation in the program has been positive because principals know it allows effective day-to-day operations to continue in their own schools while mentor support from a partner school is provided.

The information presented here has evolved over the past twelve years through a process involving research, best practices, and practical experience. That experience has been the catalyst for *Principal Mentoring: A Safe, Simple, and Supportive Approach.* Every aspect of the program process will be presented in a simple format without excessive detail to allow the reader to quickly digest the concept, and perhaps the research methods, and to permit development of a personalized district mentor-mentee program that encourages the growth of neophyte school leaders in small (including rural) and large school districts.

> It is sometimes difficult to understand the complexity of keeping things simple.
>
> —CJW

# Advocating for the Beginning Principal    **1**

**F**or several years, Albuquerque principals and district administrators realized that the school principalship was becoming increasingly more stressful and demanding. District expectations, federal guidelines, complex budgeting processes, at-risk students, dysfunctional families, increased violence, drugs, teen pregnancies, weapons on campus, a litigious society, and demands and expectations of *No Child Left Behind* made the principalship an exceptionally challenging experience. At the same time, some districts have made positive adjustments in teachers' salaries. Those adjustments may have taken away the financial incentive for teachers to become principals: less stress and a shorter contract for about the same money can be justifiable reasons for teachers not pursuing demanding principalships.

For the novice principal, there is often a difficult transition from the classroom or from an assistant principalship position. Increasingly, educators are seriously considering the challenges of the principalship before pursuing that step in their careers. Fewer applicants are available for consideration as school leaders; administrative positions are advertised frequently when no qualified candidate responds. It has become challenging for school districts to retain experienced principals. These are some of the reasons why mentor support for principals is essential and increasingly popular.

## WHY MENTORING IN OUR DISTRICT?

The Albuquerque Public Schools District and some active principals recognized those concerns. The Albuquerque Extra Support for Principals advisory board sought principal input about generating a new principal mentor program. The board determined that practicing administrators did not want more activities that would be a distraction from their own school responsibilities. As one principal reflected, "We are already called away from our schools enough by the district. We don't need another program that will add to the problem. I don't have the time as it is. If you can provide a simple program that will not demand a lot of my time, I will support it." Recognizing that time was an important issue and that beginning principals would not always feel comfortable openly expressing their frustrations or asking a question that a supervisor might perceive to be naïve, the advisory board felt a responsibility to become an advocate for the new principals. The mentor advisory board began developing the "Safe, Simple, and Supportive" concept that has become the heart of the Albuquerque principal mentor program.

It was clear that the program must maintain a **safe** environment for both mentees and mentors; nothing in the program would be implemented that could compromise the trust or dignity of the participants. To keep the process **simple,** principal involvement would be on the most basic level possible. Mentors and mentees were expected to commit 95 percent of their mentoring time addressing the needs and concerns of the mentee. The remaining 5 percent of time spent on mentoring would be devoted to mentor training and professional development. District-level administrative and management training were not part of the mentor-mentee program, although the district provided all the mandatory training opportunities for new principals. The mentor was encouraged to assist the mentee with clarifications, explanations, or resolutions to the training sessions the mentee attended. In some instances, the mentor would be invited to attend the training sessions as a resource. **Support** would remain the major reason for the existence of the program. The program is designed to provide an experienced principal who will commit to being available when the mentee needs to ask a question, seek advice, or just share or vent. The intent of the program is to help minimize the stress and frustration many new principals experience and to provide positive support. This program should help with principal retention. Information and statistics reflected in the ten-year program study on ESP (1995–2005) are found in this volume, Chapter 7.

In reviewing recent research conducted by the National Association of Elementary School Principals, superintendents from across the nation were asked to identify the primary factors that discouraged qualified teachers from pursuing a principalship. Their responses indicated that the factors were compensation 58 percent, time 25 percent, and stress 23 percent (Guterman, 2007).

- **Compensation** is not always commensurate with the additional commitment of time and responsibility. Because there is little difference between an experienced teacher's salary and a beginning principal's salary, it could be difficult for some qualified educators to justify pursuing a career as a principal. In some situations, a senior teacher seeking a principal position might be taking a cut in salary (calculating the pay differential on the additional responsibilities and time spent on the job). Some have been willing to accept the challenge, but many cannot justify the disparities. They often return to the classroom after a year or two in the principalship (Villani, 2006, p. 6).

- **Time** has always been a major concern. It is not uncommon for a principal to work ten to twelve hours a day on a regular basis. Dr. Susan Villani reflects, "Principals leaving the profession often say that they want a life outside the principalship. . . . How unfortunate that people's expanding expectations of principals may be driving away some of the individuals that schools most need to attract and retain and may be contributing to the shrinking pool of candidates" (Villani, 2006, p. 7). The time issue will be addressed in depth in Chapter 9.
- **Stress** becomes part of the job. With *No Child Left Behind* mandates and standards, jobs can be threatened if school performance declines. The feeling of loneliness and isolation can become a real issue for some, leading to increased stress. The stress factor will be discussed in Chapter 10.

## THE ANATOMY OF A BEGINNING PRINCIPAL

Educators usually begin thinking of becoming a principal while still in the classroom or in other related areas in education. They are often the ones to step forward to volunteer for additional assignments and will accept additional responsibilities within the school or district by serving on or by chairing committees. Principals and other supervisors may work with them to encourage their pursuits of administrative certification.

An aspiring principal working toward certification or licensure may take advantage of an opportunity to leave the classroom for a midlevel district position (possibly as an instructional leader or a curriculum specialist) to gain additional experience. As administrative certification or licensure requirements are achieved, attention may be directed toward more administrative roles in a school.

After the principalship appointment is acquired, reality sets in. Being responsible for the school will have an impact as the new principal realizes this is truly a new and lonely frontier; feelings of isolation may—and often do—occur. Why does anyone aspire to become a principal? What are some of the positive reasons considered by educators for wanting to become a principal? Each person must be driven by personal motives. The following are some reasons educators might consider a principalship:

1. Some see it as a stage in the professional growth and development process.

2. Others see it as an opportunity to reach beyond the classroom, to make a positive difference, or to promote leadership.

3. Some educators view it as a stepping-stone to other administrative positions.

4. An inspiration could be the desire to design a role as an instructional leader.

5. Honor and prestige of the position could be an incentive.

6. Some will accept a principalship just to increase their monthly paycheck, even though the responsibility and workload may be disproportionate to the additional compensation.

Whatever the reason or rationale, aspirants want to accept the challenge. One focus for a school district should be to provide opportunities and encouragement for potential leaders; a program or process should be in place that will encourage qualified teachers to strongly consider the principalship. Research may reflect practices that support and encourage pursuit of administrative certification. Currently, programs are in place that are as simple as grooming and encouraging strong teacher candidates or supporting teachers who are pursuing administrative certification. Some districts find ways to compensate individuals for pursuing administrative training. Grant money or leaves of absence for aspiring administrators are often used to support these programs.

Some attention is given to the use of district grants or universities to immerse administrative candidates in induction programs rather than in theory classes. Research supports the concept that practical experience under direct guidance is much more effective than an academic classroom approach (Bloom, Castagna, Moir, & Warren, 2005). New leaders are hired without special grooming or practical experience. Those leaders can become strong administrators, but they are also more susceptible to mistakes. Providing a strong support system can help prevent or preclude major issues from arising.

## PROFESSIONAL ORGANIZATIONS

Professional organizations should be considered one of the strongest advocates for the principalship. From the beginning, new principals should be encouraged to join their national, state, and local organizations. The research data and best practices shared through membership become invaluable to principals as they embark on their careers. (Membership can be obtained by contacting the National Association of Secondary School Principals or the National Association of Elementary School Principals or state and local principal organizations.)

## SCENARIO: SHARING THE WEALTH

Carl had been a sixth-grade teacher for three years. He was conscientious and enjoyed his situation. Ray, Carl's principal, had been observing Carl's performance and attitude and concluded that he had potential for becoming a school leader.

One morning Ray met Carl in the hall and suggested that he might want to consider pursuing a principalship. During the discussion, Ray offered to involve Carl in administrative practices at the school. He also suggested that Carl become more involved in serving on or chairing school- and district-level committees. Carl was given additional school responsibilities, including that of head teacher, which implied responsibility when Ray was off campus. This situation continued for three years. During that time, Carl pursued his administrative certification at the local university.

One afternoon after school, Ray called Carl into his office to introduce him to another principal, Ken. Ken's school was nearby. Ray and Ken were good friends and collaborated on a regular basis. Ray began the conversation with an apologetic tone in his voice, wanting to reassure Carl that what he was about to suggest was in his best interest.

Ray told Carl that he wanted him to transfer to Ken's school for the coming year. He indicated that he and Ken had discussed the situation and had concluded that working for a different principal would provide more opportunities for growth. On that advice, Carl agreed to the transfer.

During Carl's second year at Ken's school, Ken was appointed to direct a new summer Head Start program. He was relieved of his school responsibilities for the second semester and recommended Carl be appointed acting principal for the remainder of the school year. Later, Carl became a principal within the district and remained in the principalship for twenty-two years.

### Scenario Conclusions

It is not just coincidence that the names of the teacher in this scenario and the author of this book are the same. This is a true account of how I was directed toward the principalship. Because of the willingness of two principals to embark on the task of instilling confidence and trust in a young teacher, they were able to help guide a career that has touched many lives.

The importance of administrators taking on the additional task of advocating for the principalship by encouraging and supporting educators is vital to the survival of the profession; principal recruitment can begin with on-site administrators. We may never realize the impact or influence we may have on the people touched by our actions and deeds. Educators have the opportunity to touch lives far more than others do because of the nature of the field of education.

## KEY POINTS

1. School- and district-level administrators should be advocates for aspiring administrators and for the beginning principal.

2. School districts provide the resources to establish an early productive principal selection process for potential leaders.

3. Districts should have programs in place that address recruitment, support, and retention.

4. An assessment of a district's philosophy might include a survey on the retention and longevity of the principals and assistant principals in the district. If most active principals and assistant principals have fewer than five years' experience, it might be worth reassessing how they are recruited, hired, and supported. District neglect of this process could have ramifications on a district's educational environment. It is difficult to move forward effectively if there is little continuity in leadership.

5. Supporting new leaders during their transitional period and providing mentored advice and extemporaneous support can promote growth beyond survival.

6. The "Safe, Simple, and Supportive" approach was designed to support the beginning principal. It is not a package that addresses all areas of concern, but it is a component of the total advocacy for the principalship.

## RECOMMENDED READING

Young, P., Sheets, J., & Knight, D. (2005). *Mentoring principals: Framework, agendas, tips, and case stories for mentors and mentees.* Thousand Oaks, CA: Corwin Press.

# The Beginning of a **2** Mentor Program

The goal in this chapter is to share concerns about the lack of support for the beginning principal, how one school district addressed the issue, and the schematic developmental process of a successful program. No evidence was found of any other school district mentoring program designed and developed by principals and for principals. The Albuquerque Public Schools (APS) process is described here, along with lessons learned and recommendations for new program development.

## APS DISTRICT DEMOGRAPHICS

Based on enrollment, the APS District is one of the thirty largest school districts in the nation. For the 2007–08 school year, the district comprised twelve high schools (with a thirteenth to open for the 2008–09 school year), thirty-two middle schools, eighty-four elementary schools, seven alternative schools, and thirty-eight charter schools. Total enrollment in the district was 93,095 students in the 2007–08 school year. Instruction is divided into three levels: elementary, middle, and high schools. Elementary school is pre-K to fifth grades, middle school is sixth to eighth grades, and high school is ninth through twelfth grades. There are seven alternative schools based on various grade combinations and focuses. The district supports thirty-eight charter schools, including eight elementary charter schools, ten middle school charter schools, and twenty high school charter schools. There are 134 principals throughout the public school district. The district-level administrative structure consists of a superintendent, three associate superintendents, two assistant superintendents, and several department directors (APS Leadership, n.d.).

Knowledge of the demographics of APS will be helpful in understanding the need and strategy for developing a successful principal mentor program. These strategies may be appropriate no matter the size or composition of the school district.

## THE BIRTH OF THE
## ALBUQUERQUE MENTOR PROGRAM

Until the early 1990s, APS did not have a principals' mentor program. If new principals needed support, they sought it as best they could. Normally, they would contact experienced principals within the district.

During the 1991–92 school year, a newly appointed elementary principal, Peter Espinosa, began contacting an experienced principal for advice, guidance, and support. This mentoring relationship continued throughout the year on an informal basis. Peter had a successful first year. Because of the mentoring relationship he experienced, he felt it would be helpful if every new principal received the support he had had with an experienced principal. Peter saw a strong need for a structured support system for new principals; he took the initiative to present his concern to the APS Principals Association (APSPA). A committee was assembled, made up of principals from all three levels, retired principals, the executive director of APSPA, community leaders, a district-level administrator, and a representative from the University of New Mexico. That committee worked together to research and survey the need for a mentor program and the ways that it could be established.

The primary goals were to provide experienced principals who would be available to serve as mentors for first-year principals and to create professional development opportunities specifically designed for the neophytes. Research and best practices were used to convince the district of the importance of such a support system. The need was established, and a proposal, including a detailed budget, was developed and presented to the administration for consideration. It was a small budget request, and the committee members felt it would be more likely to be approved if they were specific about how the money would be utilized.

## BUDGET JUSTIFICATION

**Exhibit 2A**

| | |
|---|---|
| *Coordinator's Salary* | The coordinator will be paid $1,000 per month in school year 1995–96 to carry out all duties and responsibilities associated with the APS mentor program. |
| | The coordinator's salary gradually increased to $1,300 per month for twelve months during the 2006–07 school year. |

| Mentor Stipends | A stipend will be given to each mentor for supporting a mentee for one year. The stipend amount for a mentor will be determined by the number of mentors involved. The amount will be no less than $500 and no more than $1,000 per year. |
|---|---|
| In-Service and Professional Development | Funds will be made available to provide mentor training and two professional development opportunities (one each semester) for interactive sessions for mentors and mentees. |
| Supplies and Materials | Funds will provide basic office supplies, materials, and printing for the program (including a mentor handbook). |
| Small Equipment | To be determined as program needs warrant. |
| Mileage | Coordinator will be reimbursed for in-district auto travel while performing the program's duties. |

In 1995, the committee was successful in receiving both philosophical and financial support from the district when the $30,000 budget was approved. The organizing committee became the advisory board. The advisory board selected the name Extra Support for Principals for the program. Roles and responsibilities were established and the program was implemented.

**Exhibit 2B**   Extra Support for Principals Mentor Program Budget

The Albuquerque mentor program 1995–96 budget compared with the 2006–07 budget.

| Budgets | 1995–96 | 2006–07 |
|---|---|---|
| Coordinator's salary | $12,000 | $15,600 |
| Mentor stipends | $10,000 | $15,600 |
| In-service and professional development | $4,000 | $6,500 |
| Supplies and printing | $2,500 | $2,000 |
| Small equipment | $500 | $500 |
| Mileage | $1,000 | $1,000 |
| Totals | $30,000 | $41,200 |

Unencumbered funds revert back to the human resources department at the end of each fiscal year. Flexibility is given to the budget control agent to transfer funds within the program if the need arises.

Misconception: It takes a lot of money to create and maintain an effective mentor program.

—CJW

## SELECTING A COORDINATOR

The next step for the advisory board was to hire a coordinator for the mentor program. The board established the list of qualifications desired for the position of coordinator. The position was not advertised; experience shows that advertising should be considered, however. Qualifications for a mentor included the following:

- Will devote the time needed with little compensation
- Will work within the approved budget
- Has knowledge of the role of principal or experience as a principal
- Is respected and shares the confidence of the district principals
- Has good communication skills
- Is skilled in human relations
- Is tactful and diplomatic
- Has the ability to procure needed resources
- Displays sound time-management skills
- Has strong organizational skills
- Reflects a positive attitude
- Is committed to promoting the principalship
- Has the desire to help professional cohorts grow professionally

This list was developed from a brainstorming activity. The intent was to recruit someone with as many of these qualities as possible. Brainstorming proved to be a good activity to begin the process of selecting a coordinator. There were two options the board considered: hire a retired principal or assign the responsibilities to an APS employee. The advisory board chose the retired principal option for two reasons. First, the staffer being considered had not been a principal. Therefore, the board considered that the person might not understand the needs of a beginning principal. Second, the board believed a retired principal would be more dedicated to the mission and would be more receptive to devote the time and energy to make the program succeed. At the time, I was a retired principal and was offered the position. I was asked to review the budget to assess the offer, and I accepted the challenge. The advisory board and the coordinator began meeting on a regular basis to develop the program.

The APS human resources department was given the responsibility of supervising the program because the

---

**A Positive Message**

By financially supporting a principal mentor program, the district sends a strong positive message: "We care about our principals and we want them to succeed. We also respect and value the experience and expertise the mentors bring to the program, and we are willing to compensate them for their contributions."

—CJW

department would have firsthand knowledge of the principal appointments as soon as they occurred. The director of staffing for human resources was assigned to be the control agent for the program's budget; the director and the coordinator would work closely to fund program needs and support.

---

**KEY POINTS**

1. The planning and presentation process for an organized mentor-mentee program is significant because it entails thinking about new directions for supporting neophyte principals.

2. Experienced principals should have a strong voice in the development and implementation of the mentor-mentee program.

3. Successful practices of delegating and empowering can be applied and should be encouraged during the presentation of any new program.

4. It is important to provide data that support the request. Although best practices are excellent resources, they do not fit in every situation, especially when thinking creatively about a different concept. No matter how strong the strategy might be, it must be adapted to the unique needs of the district.

5. The superintendent and other administrators must share in the vision of mentor support.

6. Once district approval is achieved, the vision of structured mentor support is close to becoming a reality.

---

## RECOMMENDED READINGS

Weingartner, C. J. (2001). "Albuquerque principals have ESP." *Principal: The principalship in crisis,* 80(4), 40–42. Alexandria, VA: National Association of Elementary School Principals.

Young, P., Sheets, J., & Knight, D. (2005). *Mentoring principals: Framework, agendas, tips, and case stories for mentors and mentees.* Thousand Oaks, CA: Corwin Press.

Zachary, L. J. (2005). *Creating a mentoring culture: The organizational guide.* San Francisco: Jossey-Bass.

# A Work in Process  **3**

This chapter is devoted to a developmental process for establishing a mentoring program's foundation. Suggestions are offered in an effort to help organize a structured program that should be helpful meeting individual districts' concerns for new principal support.

## THE FIRST STAGES OF DEVELOPMENT

As the program began, the first tasks of the coordinator and the advisory board were to structure the process and determine a program style. The advisory board and coordinator were in total agreement that they would

- Avoid overwhelming the participants with needless meetings or paperwork
- Respect principals' time
- Maintain a safe environment for mentees
- Involve the mentee in the mentor selection process
- Keep program focus on supporting the new principal
- Avoid hidden agendas

With ground rules established, the coordinator developed drafts for segments of the program that included (1) a vision statement, (2) a mission statement, (3) program guidelines, (4) job descriptions for both coordinator and mentor, and (5) the program process. To conserve time, the coordinator sent copies of each draft to each advisory board member for review. During the program planning meetings, the current draft would be discussed and revised. The goal was to produce a program handbook for principals and assistant principals so they would become knowledgeable about the program. Each district-level administrator received a final copy. Different areas that the board felt needed to be formalized in order to establish a program foundation included the preceding numerical listing and a process for delivering support.

## VISION AND MISSION STATEMENTS

Vision and mission statements represent examples of the process developed in the organizational planning during program inception. Both vision and mission statements have evolved over the years and are the result of twelve years of collaboration between the advisory board and district administrators. These are suggestions or ideas that can be used in program development. Vision and mission statements are critical parts of the developmental process. They help identify the direction and establish program goals. More information on how to develop vision and mission statements can be located in the documents *Mission Expert: Creating Effective Mission and Vision Statements (n.d.)* and *Example Mission Statement (n.d.)*.

### Vision Statement

Take a moment to develop your vision statement. First, take a look at this example.

It is a shared belief of the district that providing a support system of experienced principals for new principals in a collegial environment will enhance the new principal's administrative and instructional leadership by providing thought-provoking questions, advice, suggestions, and recommendations in a professional development environment. Furthermore, it is hoped that mentor support will provide a positive experience that will be influential in the decision to make the principalship a life-long career.

Given your present situation and assuming that you are interested in pursuing a mentor program for your district, what would your vision statement include?

_____

_____

_____

_____

_____

### Mission Statement

Take a moment to develop your mission statement. First, take a look at this example.

The purpose of the mentor program is for all new principals to have collegial contact that will provide opportunities to inquire, discuss, probe, and resolve issues while promoting a positive leadership role and to utilize the expertise of veteran principals in a safe, simple, and supportive environment during the transitional first year.

Given your present situation and assuming that you are interested in pursuing a mentor program for your district, what would your mission statement need to include?

_____

_____

_____

_____

_____

## PROGRAM GUIDELINES

- The principal mentor program will be a collaboration of the Albuquerque Public Schools Principals Association (APSPA) and the Albuquerque Public Schools (APS) District.
- The district has designated the executive director for human resources to oversee the principal mentor program.
- The director of staffing for human resources has been designated as the budget control agent for the principal mentor program.
- The principal mentor program has been given the title Extra Support for Principals.
- The Extra Support for Principals advisory board will advise the program coordinator and the program control agent.
- The advisory board will meet on a regular basis during the school year unless the advisory board deems it unnecessary to do so.
- The advisory board will make recommendations to the executive director for human resources and to the control agent for the program coordinator position.
- The program coordinator will keep the advisory board informed as to the happenings and progress on the principal mentor program.
- The program coordinator will work closely with the program control agent and the district project manager.
- New principals will be identified as those who have been assigned to the position of principal for the first time. The principal mentor program will be offered to first-year principals, principals changing levels for the first time, and experienced principals hired from other districts.
- New principals will be assigned to the program based on the timing of their appointments.

- The principal mentor program is a voluntary program.
- District superintendents will be involved in the mentor screening process.
- A list of potential mentors will be developed from this process.
- New principals will be able to recommend mentors.
- The program coordinator makes mentor assignments from the approved list.
- The advisory board will be informed of the mentor-mentee assignments.
- The district-level administrators will be informed of the mentor-mentee assignments.
- Mentors should be selected from the same level of the mentee's principalship (elementary–elementary, middle school–middle school, high school–high school). Exceptions will be considered, but must first be approved by the superintendents or advisory board.
- Approved active-level principals will be given first consideration for a mentorship. However, retired principals who have been retired for three years or less will also be considered. The board or a superintendent must approve exceptions from the normal selection process.
- Mentors will receive a stipend for carrying out their responsibilities. (Stipends may vary from year to year depending on the number of mentors and the budget allocation.)
- A mentee will generate one mentor stipend.
- Except on special occasions, one mentor will support one mentee. Exceptions will be approved by the ESP board or a superintendent.
- A mentorship will last one calendar year from the time of the appointment.

## JOB DESCRIPTIONS

### Coordinator

- Will meet new principals shortly after the neophytes have been appointed
- Will interview new principals to
  a. become acquainted with them and their administrative style,
  b. identify their focus and concerns,
  c. obtain input on areas of in-service training, and
  d. discuss possible mentors.
- Will coordinate mentor-mentee assignments
- Will meet with mentors to discuss responsibilities
- Will provide training opportunities for mentors
- Will maintain regular communication with the mentoring relationships

- Will meet with the advisory board on any concerns or uncertainties
- Will identify meeting places, times, and agendas
- Will coordinate in-service training
- Will collaborate on the hiring of presenters for any in-service programs
- Will collaborate, meet with, and plan with the in-service presenters
- Will coordinate publications, i.e., flyers, training manuals or handbooks, newsletters, and other forms of written communication
- Will intervene in the event a conflict between a mentor-mentee should occur
- Will work closely with the control agent and program manager

## Mentor

The mentor is a critical partner in the success of the mentor-mentee relationship. The mentor shares the responsibilities for the new administrator's (mentee's) developmental journey by providing support, advice, and vision. Both mentor and new principal become partners in learning, with the mentor providing opportunities for thought-provoking experiences as well as insight into the normal operations of the school environment. A climate of trust permits the mentee to feel safe in considering new perspectives and behaviors. Most important, both must understand that the freedom to fail is a precondition for growth and development.

The level of success of the mentorship is related directly to the mentor's job description. The responsibilities of the mentor include the following:

- Establishing initial contact with the mentee to provide support whenever the mentee needs help.
- Establishing a sense of commitment.
- Whenever possible, attending scheduled meetings and in-service programs, e.g., program orientations or celebrations, and luncheon and in-service meetings.
- Establishing a routine for communicating contact by phone, e-mail, electronic communication devices, established contact meetings, or at in-service meetings. (Communication is very important, but opportunities for communicating will vary depending on need and level of support. A mentor should make contact with the mentee at least every other week to check on progress.)
- Communicating or interacting with the mentee at least three hours a month in order to have an effective support system for the mentor.
- Being available for advice, for support, to share experiences, and to listen to the concerns of the mentee. Mentors must clarify that no one has all the answers and that the mentor is not the one to solve the mentee's problems.

- Fostering a personal environment that encourages creativity, intellectual freedom, experimentation, or risk taking.
- Helping the mentee develop self-confidence.
- Being willing to discuss professional growth of the mentee, as well as on-the-job issues and conflicts.
- Acting sometimes as a mentor and sometimes as a cheerleader.
- Providing constructive feedback and encouragement.
- Participating in the end-of-the-year program evaluations.

## PROGRAM PROCESS

When establishing a mentorship, the coordinator will do the following:

- Make initial contact with the new principal to set up an appointment to congratulate and establish a meeting for the initial visit.
- Meet with the new principal to explain the mentor program and to
  a. discuss mentor selection process,
  b. answer questions about the program,
  c. discuss the mentor handbook,
  d. discuss orientation training,
  e. discuss content briefings and in-service opportunities,
  f. consider areas of focus,
  g. give mentee the opportunity to share concerns or areas of need,
  h. discuss administrative styles, and
  i. discuss possible mentor assignment.
- Make initial contact by phone with the potential mentor to
  a. inform the potential mentor that he or she has been requested as a mentor,
  b. offer congratulations and the mentorship position to the experienced principal selected, and
  c. if the potential mentor accepts the opportunity, to make an appointment and meet with the mentor.
- Meet with mentor selected to
  a. explain the mentor program and responsibilities,
  b. discuss the handbook,
  c. answer questions about the program,
  d. create an awareness of a time commitment,
  e. discuss mentor and in-service training as part of the commitment,
  f. inform mentor of the compensation for time and expertise,
  g. alert mentor to a required mentor training session,

    h. discuss "Mentor Job Description" and "Suggestions for Mentors Working with New Principals" located in the handbook, and

    i. share areas of concerns mentioned by the mentee.

## A TOTAL SUPPORT SYSTEM FOR NEW PRINCIPALS

It is important to realize that a safe, simple, and supportive mentor program might be difficult to develop if it is not separated from the supervisory aspects of the school district. Some districts will utilize a mentor program for problem-solving issues rather than for the growth and development of a new administrator. Districts accept the responsibility to inform, supervise, evaluate, and train new administrators. They also recognize difficulties that newly appointed principals may face. Knowing how to proceed while allowing the new principal (mentee) the opportunity to develop into an effective leader is the challenge. If the approach is reactive, the outcome could be that the opportunities to improve a neophyte's leadership skills may diminish. The district must provide a total support system to benefit the district goals and objectives while providing new principals the opportunity to grow into productive leaders who will want to continue to lead.

    In 1999, discussions with the superintendents led to the development of the New Principal Total Support System (Exhibit 3A).

**Exhibit 3A**    New Principal Total Support System

Supervision      Mentoring

Training
Coaching
Operation issues
Evaluation
Correction plans
Content briefings

Professional development
In-service

One on one
Safe, simple, supportive
Principal-directed
support

*Source:* Designed and developed by Carl J. Weingartner.

In this newly developed system, supervision was the responsibility of the district and mentoring was the responsibility of the mentor principals and mentor program. Some joint professional development and in-service opportunities were accomplished through collaborative efforts. The mentor program took on a focus that included coordinated involvement with superintendents and their designees who conducted training sessions on critical areas of need. Sessions were well organized and beneficial for both mentees and the mentors. Department directors were responsible for the training in different areas of expertise. For example, the director of human resources had training sessions on staff evaluation procedures.

In 2004, APS further strengthened support for beginning principals. The district created a position of project manager to focus on training new principals. Along with other responsibilities, the project manager position was to be responsible for providing opportunities for all newly appointed principals and experienced principals new to the district to attend content briefings on critical operational topics such as staff evaluations, internal audits, harassment issues, activity funds guidelines, special education issues, instruction, state standards, testing, and *No Child Left Behind* mandates. Content briefings were scheduled on a regular basis for two hours twice a month with mandatory attendance of all mentees.

The project manager and mentor coordinator worked independently, but shared information and coordinated activities to avoid scheduling conflicts and program replication. The mentoring process provided support in a nonthreatening, supportive environment, while the content briefings were directed at the operational issues that principals must know in order to comply with district policies and procedures. The overlap encompassed the area of professional development. In some cases, mentors were invited to the content briefings to support their mentees; in every case, they were invited to attend the professional development activities. In both situations, mentors might offer advice, direction, and clarification to some of the topics. This concept of total support focuses on both the individual needs of the mentee and on district compliance issues. Through much change, evolution, and four administrations, the mentor program maintained the safe, simple, and supportive concept. The Venn diagram in Exhibit 3A has helped to maintain the compatibility between the two different organizational structures. Changes could be made to adapt this concept to the needs of the individual school district.

## KEY POINTS

1. APS mentor program has had its share of issues. Because of the simplicity of the program, however, it never became a managerial monstrosity. The program has grown and improved from its inception. Knowledge and experience gained through the years could benefit anyone contemplating a mentor program.

2. The APS district and the mentor program are fortunate to have leaders who have displayed visionary skills while addressing the issue of a support system for new principals.

3. In recent years, the superintendents have accepted responsibility to provide the operational training component while maintaining a safe mentoring environment for beginning principals. Both the district and mentor programs have been able to build on a concept and develop it into a total package that provides the support system that is invaluable for beginning principals.

4. Creating an awareness of the need for a joint district and mentor program should encourage every district developing a mentor program to consider the inclusion of a joint support concept.

5. Organizing, planning, researching, writing, meeting, revising, and finalizing the fundamental foundation of the mentor program will help ensure success.

6. A realization that each district or area is unique creates a need for review of operating programs and an analysis of district needs.

7. Vision and mission statements are the most critical part of the planning: those statements help establish program goals. It is necessary to focus on the individual district needs.

8. The development of program guidelines, processes, and job descriptions tends to add creditability to a program and provides a formal design to encourage commitment from both mentees and mentors. It also provides a comfort zone for the mentee knowing that asking for help or advice when it is needed will not be imposing on their mentor.

## RECOMMENDED READINGS

Mission Expert. (n.d.). Creating effective mission and vision statements. http://www.mission-vision-ebook.com/.

Nightingale-Conant. (n.d.) Example mission statement. http://www.nightingale.com/mission_select.aspx

# Program Implementation

# 4

Certain steps for implementing the philosophy of a safe, simple, and supportive approach to principal mentoring are critical to the process of inducting new principals into the program and supporting them throughout the year. Key components of this mentor model are administrative support, the selection of an advisory board, a budget that is in place, and design of the basic program. Best practices for implementing a mentor-mentee program are discussed in the following five steps.

## STEP 1. THE PROCESS BEGINS

The process of involvement begins when the human resources department contacts the mentor coordinator about recent new principal appointments. Human resources shares basic information about those appointees with the coordinator (names, phone numbers, professional experience, last positions held, and the official date for assuming new responsibilities).

The coordinator of the mentor program promptly makes positive contact with the appointees by phone. A newly appointed principal often has heard about the mentor-mentee program and is receptive to its goals and the support system it offers. If the neophyte is not familiar with the program, a brief explanation is given, along with the reassurance that a deeper discussion can follow. The coordinator informs the newly appointed principal of the approved list of mentors from which to select, and asks the new principal to consider the choice of potential mentors. A date and time is established for the initial meeting with the coordinator. Congratulatory comments and encouragement might be expressed again at the end of the first contact.

## STEP 2. THE INITIAL COORDINATOR-MENTEE MEETING

Precautions must be taken to ensure that the new principal, who has just accepted new and major responsibilities, is not overwhelmed. The newly appointed principal may feel excited, isolated, or even frightened. The neophyte may even experience self-doubt and question whether the decision to accept these responsibilities was a wise one. The initial meeting between the coordinator and the appointee needs to be positive and provide a level of comfort and reassurance. It is important to emphasize that knowledgeable, stress-free support is available from an experienced principal (the mentor).

This initial meeting can be approached as a celebration. Upon visiting with the new principal, the coordinator might present a congratulatory card or flower along with a tangible memento that will encourage a smile. In the Albuquerque Public School (APS) program, it is a congratulatory rose and a coffee mug commemorating the appointment. The mug caption reads, "I have ESP," in honor of the Extra Support for Principals program. (The mugs are provided by one of the program's business partners who specialize in school pictures and personalized items.) The coordinator then makes the transition to the value of the mentoring program and the support it can provide.

During this first session, a copy of the mentor program handbook is presented to the mentee and basic aspects of the program are covered. It is stressed that the program is a support system with no hidden agenda. The coordinator even states that if the program is increasing the level of stress, it is no longer a support system and steps should be taken to minimize the stress it is creating. Program resources are designed to provide additional support in this exciting first year. The coordinator also points out that the mentee and mentor will control 95 percent of the involvement of the mentor program, and that the program is based on the needs of the mentee. The other 5 percent of the program includes an informal get-acquainted social, a mentor training session, two in-service or professional development opportunities, and an end-of-the-year evaluation. This informal interview helps gather knowledge about issues or concerns the new principal might express. During this interview, the coordinator might also discuss some focus on mentor support.

The topic of mentor selection is addressed after the list of approved and available mentors is presented. The development of the mentor list involves the superintendents or designated district-level administrators. Those responsible review a list of every principal with five or more years of experience; they have the discretion to purge any name from the list. The superintendents may add principals who might have fewer than five years experience if those principals are known to have strong mentor or leadership qualities. The purged list then becomes the approved mentor list. The mentee is encouraged to provide the coordinator with three names from the list in priority order. The mentee may have an experienced principal in mind. If the recommended principal is on the mentor list, an effort will be made to accommodate the mentee. If the first choice is not on the approved list, the coordinator will ask the mentee to consider others. As mentors are assigned, their names are removed from the list of available mentors. During the meeting wrap-up, the new principal is told that the next step will be to offer the mentorship to the selected principal.

## STEP 3. CONFERRING WITH THE MENTOR

After the initial contact with the newly appointed principal, it is the coordinator's responsibility to confer with the potential mentor. A brief phone call or personal visit will be sufficient to establish a dialogue. During this conversation, the principal (potential mentor) is informed of the request. If the principal is willing to accept the position, the coordinator shares information about the mentee. If the mentor accepts, an appointment is established at the convenience of the new mentor, and the coordinator expresses appreciation for the mentor's willingness to support the mentee. If the mentor does not accept, the coordinator notifies the mentee and proceeds to the second choice. It is noteworthy that over the history of the APS mentor program there have only been two principals who have declined the opportunity to mentor and only for a specific year. Both had served as mentors before but had committed to other responsibilities for the year and did not feel they could contribute the time needed to be an effective mentor. Those reasons were justifiable and appreciated.

The meeting between the coordinator and the mentor begins in much the same way as the one with the newly appointed principal (mentee). The mentor is presented a rose and a commemorative coffee mug similar to the one presented earlier. The rose is an expression of appreciation instead of celebration, and the coffee mug, as in the first meeting, is a memento commemorating involvement in the program.

The coordinator shares with the mentor some of the information gathered during the informal interview with the mentee. Any information about specific areas of support, concerns, or frustrations would be addressed. The coordinator informs the mentor that he or she and the mentee will be in control of 95 percent of the mentee's program, and that the program is based on the needs of the mentee. The other 5 percent of the program includes the celebratory, social, and other sessions mentioned above. The mentor handbook is reviewed, with certain topics highlighted throughout the discussion. These topics are "Getting the Most Out of the ESP Mentor Program," "Mentoring vs. Coaching," "Time

Management: Timelines and Calendars," and "Suggestions for Mentors Working with New Principals" (Weingartner, 2006, pp. 10–30). Mentors are encouraged to read the topics in the handbook and to reflect on how they will impact individual mentoring responsibilities.

Other suggestions and ideas are addressed during this session. They include, but are not limited to, the following:

1. The coordinator encourages the mentor to think of ways to celebrate the appointment. Suggestions are a card, a bouquet of flowers, a box of candy, a tangible memento, or a lunch with the mentee.

2. The mentor and mentee must establish a communication protocol with which each feels comfortable. Committing to a definite routine is strongly suggested. Best practices have shown that if there is not a commitment to communicate on a regular basis, the mentoring process tends to fall through the cracks as the year progresses. The established communication system should include a minimum of three hours of contact per month. If the mentor has not heard from the neophyte for a two-week period, the mentor should contact the mentee. These suggestions also serve as benchmarks to help determine if program goals are being met.

3. Find opportunities for the mentor and mentee to become better acquainted. Encourage the veteran to share some personal feelings and background, to discuss critical areas of support and need, and to develop goals and objectives for the year.

4. Alert the mentor about the mentor training session and the schedule. (Encourage mentors to attend the session if they have not recently attended the training.)

5. Inform the experienced principal of meetings that occur throughout the year. Provide dates whenever possible. Those dates will include three activities: a mentor training session and at least two sessions on new principal content briefings. Some content briefings are designed by school district staff to include mentor participation and support. It is comforting to most mentors to know they will be expected to attend only five or six mentoring activities throughout the year. The rest of the commitment is directed toward supporting the mentee.

The experienced principal (mentor) is encouraged to contact the new principal as soon as possible to congratulate the mentee and to convey enthusiasm about the program and about the sharing that will take place throughout the year. Once an appointment between the mentor and mentee has been established, the third step is complete.

## STEP 4. THE PLANNING SESSION

The mentor now takes charge. Shortly after conferring with the coordinator, the mentor should contact the mentee. Again, a congratulatory greeting would be appropriate. By expressing appreciation for having been selected and the honor it implies, the experienced administrator can begin establishing that first level of trust and confidence. Conversation about the mentee's appointment can lead to establishing a regular or specific time when the two can meet.

How well the mentor and mentee know each other can have a bearing on how this first meeting will be conducted. If they are meeting for the first time, a visit to the new principal's school might be appropriate. If they know one another, a celebratory breakfast or lunch might be in order. Basing the decision on the comfort level of the mentee is important; the two should agree on the most comfortable setting for the mentee.

The purpose of the first meeting is to discuss the needs and concerns of the beginning principal, to establish goals and objectives, to develop a plan for support, and to create a communication protocol that will meet the needs of both. This establishes the groundwork for a collaborative relationship that will last throughout the year (and hopefully beyond).

## STEP 5. THE OTHER 5 PERCENT

Steps 1–4 make up approximately 95 percent of the time involved in the APS mentor program. The additional 5 percent includes the supportive activities and communications throughout the year. A comprehensive process and timeline for the remaining portion of the mentoring process includes the following:

*Handbook Distribution and Other Communications.* Beginning in August of each year, a revised and updated mentoring handbook is distributed to all principals, assistant principals, district administrators, APS board of education members, and the ESP advisory board. The goal is to keep potential participants informed of program purposes and goals.

- Bimonthly newsletters are published to keep everyone informed about events and happenings within the program, i.e., new principal appointments, mentor assignments, and upcoming activities and events. Providing opportunities for praise, appreciation, or recognition are important to the process. Lois Zachary encourages newsletters as part of the total communication process: "A strategy might therefore be to create a monthly mentoring newsletter for those participating in a mentoring activity" (Zachary, 2005, p. 140). In addition, the ESP newsletter has been distributed to approximately 75 individuals, school-district personnel, university professors, and authors because of the interest they have shown in the program. This distribution includes regions throughout the United States, Canada, and the United Kingdom.

*Mentor Training.* In the first few weeks of school, a scheduled training session should be conducted for mentors. Timing will be in direct relationship to the final date of the principal appointments. If several positions are unfilled, considerations may be given to delaying the training until the majority of the positions are filled.

- The training is basic in nature and is usually accomplished within a morning or afternoon session. The focus of the training is based on the "Suggestions for Mentors Working With Mentees" in Chapter 8 of this volume. It is an open forum where discussion and sharing of experiences are encouraged. Nationally known mentoring experts have been used sometimes to share their experiences and ideas with the principals. Although these occasions are voluntary, an effort is made to encourage all district principals to attend. These activities have been supported strongly in the APS program. A school district should consider providing mentoring experts as resources.

*The Celebration or Social Activity.* After school has begun and a normal routine has been established, new leaders and their mentors are invited to attend a celebratory or social activity. This event usually is held in mid-October after most positions have been filled and mentor matches have been made.

- The activity is usually held in the late afternoon after school dismissal. The location is always away from the school environment, normally at a hotel conference room or a condominium clubhouse, depending on the size of the group. The invitation list includes the mentees, mentors, advisory board, and the district administration. (The APS board of education has chosen to meet with the new principals at a different time and location.)
- The program is about two hours long, usually from 4:00 to 6:00 in the afternoon. A social hour with refreshments begins the activity. This is a time when everyone has the opportunity to visit with old acquaintances and to meet the new principals. (Refreshments are provided by the business partners.)
- The second part of the program is the celebration. It begins with the introductions of district administrators and advisory board members who are present. As introductions are made, each is encouraged to take a moment to express congratulations to the new leaders. After recognizing and appreciating the support of the

business partners, the mentees and mentors are given time to introduce themselves and share their early feelings or experiences since being appointed. This is a rewarding opportunity; most mentees express appreciation for the support they are receiving, while the experienced principals reflect on the honor of having been selected as a mentor. Often humorous experiences are shared. At the end of the session, a drawing is conducted for gift certificates to popular restaurants. (These, too, are provided by the business partners.) The whole process in designed to be informal, and is a time for celebration.

*Professional Development.* There are two luncheon or professional development opportunities scheduled within the year's activities, one each semester. The first is planned for December, while the other is planned for February. Mentees and mentors are included. Topics may vary, but the focus is on areas that will enrich professional growth, i.e., "Effective Time Management" or "Enhancing a Positive School Climate." Sometimes the sessions address the "First 60 Days of School" or the "Final 60 Days of School." The program delivery includes a presentation, followed by round-table interaction between mentees and mentors. (Round tables with eight seats are suggested.) Program topics are often based on the suggestions and needs of the new principals involved.

- These sessions are often conducted in a hotel conference room. Lunch is provided, thanks to business partners. The sessions normally begin at 12:30 and end about 4:00 PM. Lunch is served from 12:30 to 1:30 PM, while the programmed activities run from 1:30 to 3:30 PM. (Starting the luncheon at 12:30 gives principals the opportunity to ensure their school lunch schedules are running smoothly before they leave campus). The final half hour is devoted to wrap-up, which includes a simple program evaluation, announcements, and drawings for gift certificates.

*Culminating Activities.* During the final six weeks of school, the coordinator visits the schools of all the participating principals, both mentees and mentors. Time is spent with the new principal (mentee) to determine the level of support received. Attempts are made to assess the level of time and stress the mentor-mentee program imposed on both the mentor and mentee as they carried out their duties and responsibilities. Each principal is encouraged to think about the positive and negative aspects of the program and the lessons learned. The Coordinator informs all participating principals that a culminating survey will be developed and that they will be asked to respond at the end of the year. In addition, the coordinator presents each participant with a framed certificate of appreciation for support and participation. (Mentors are reminded they will be receiving their second-semester stipend for their mentoring efforts.) This concludes the year's activities. Although the formal program has concluded, the mentees are encouraged to continue their relationship with their mentors on an informal basis.

## KEY POINTS

1. A mentor program must be adapted to meet the needs of the school district. There are many factors that impact the development of a program. The administration of the program, the support system in place, the number of new principals involved, individual district needs, district size and geographical boundaries, and funding are all key components that should be considered.

2. Sharing this induction process is an attempt to encourage a district to have the district program focus on a realization that a new principal (mentee) may start the new situation filled with anxiety.

3. Neophytes appreciate the opportunity to have a support system that does not have a hidden agenda or outlandish expectations.

4. A mentor program needs to be designed to provide a support system, help relieve stress, and assist in professional growth. It also needs to be designed with the idea that the beginning principal will feel positive about his or her new role and want to pursue the challenges. New appointees know they have district obligations and responsibilities for which they will be held accountable. If those areas can be addressed through other district channels rather than by the mentor program, the safe, simple, and supportive program components can be more effectively maintained.

5. Each mentee must feel supported in a manner that encourages professional growth beyond survival.

6. Assessing program procedures may assist in establishing a process that is most appropriate for a specific district's goals.

7. One should not assume that mentoring in itself is the solution to every problem the leader will encounter. It does play a role in the total process, however. Even with a total support approach, there are no guarantees of total achievement or perfection. Daresh (2001) observes, "Mentoring is an important part of effective administrator professional development. But you are alerted here to the fact that it cannot be viewed as the panacea that will solve all problems facing leaders" (xii). Keep in mind that the focus should be on the messages conveyed and not just on the activities presented.

## RECOMMENDED READINGS

Bloom, G., Castagna, C., Moir, E., & Warren, B. (2005). *Blended coaching: Skills and strategies to support principal development.* Thousand Oaks, CA: Corwin Press.

Daresh, J. C. (2001). *Leaders helping leaders: A practical guide to administrative mentoring.* Thousand Oaks, CA: Corwin Press.

Zachary, L. J. (2000). *The mentors' guide: Facilitating effective learning relationships.* San Francisco: Jossey-Bass.

# Simple Program   5
# Enhancements Make
# a Difference

---

**B**oth mentor programs and individual mentors require positive attitudes, knowledge, experience, attention to detail, and patience. In addition, small acts of appreciation and recognition can improve the morale of a neophyte administrator. Ways to promote a positive climate and attitude are many.

## CONGRATULATE

For beginning principals, this appointment is probably one of the most exciting events of their careers. It is important for others to acknowledge the achievement. The coordinator should officially congratulate the new principal in person as well as with the presentation of some sort of tangible memento such as a card, a bouquet of flowers, a box of candy, or a lunch with the mentee. These and other options could help create a memorable, positive induction.

The next level of acknowledgment and congratulations should come from the assigned mentor. Establishing trust and confidence should be the first order of business. It is important to convey the message that the mentor program is available to provide help and support. (Other principals not directly connected to the mentoring process also could be encouraged to contact and congratulate the new principals.)

## CELEBRATE

Celebrating the appointment of a new principal may not seem like a big step in the establishment of a mentor relationship, but it is. The objective of congratulations is to create a positive atmosphere of support. A plan can be developed to let new principals know they are enthusiastically accepted as part of the principalship team. Celebration should come from the district level as well as from the individual mentors. Resourceful mentors could think of other creative options that might be especially appropriate for a given celebratory opportunity.

The mentor program coordinator could plan a celebration or social activity some afternoon or evening for all newly appointed principals. Although principal appointments are made throughout the year, most are completed by late August. Therefore, this activity could take place in the first two months of the school year to incorporate the largest number of new appointees. Obviously, if a district is small and there are only one or two new principals, adjustments can be made.

Celebrating levels of accomplishments throughout the year, too, can be a positive motivational tool. Sharing successes promotes confidence and self-esteem in both mentee and mentor; celebrating a successful first year can be most rewarding. The program coordinator could play an active role by presenting each participant with a certificate or a memento commemorating successful participation in program.

## COMMUNICATE

Communication is a significant component of an effective mentor program. Establishing a systemwide communication network helps sustain program continuity and purpose. Periodic mentoring publications or newsletters can inform the program participants as well as the school district at large. These documents are also a way to keep everyone informed of upcoming events or reports and can serve as an avenue to congratulate and celebrate appointments made throughout the year, keeping in mind that individuals who are informed about new appointments are more likely to be supportive of the program. Lois Zachary (2005) observes, "Communication makes some mentoring efforts more successful than others. A mentoring culture has an effective strategic communication plan that it regularly implements and monitors. As a consequence, executives, managers, and coworkers all understand what mentoring is and know how to get involved in it" (p. 53).

A mentor handbook should be informative and should be distributed to all administrators in the district. With computer technology, publishing a periodical or a handbook is not overwhelming, and the time spent is well worth the investment. Much of the information provided in this volume could be used as a guideline for developing a basic handbook. Other information of interest such as district timelines and deadlines, school calendars, and reminders can help make it more useful for principals. Another suggestion to encourage reading might be to insert a cover letter indicating that someone—for example, the coordinator—has autographed one or two copies of the document somewhere within. Holders of these copies could win a motivational prize or gift certificate.

It is important that a mentor-mentee team establish a communication routine at the beginning of their relationship. There should be an agreement on a minimal amount of contact time per month; the mentor program recommends three hours minimum. Methods of communication will vary with each team. There are many options beyond personal meetings: phone calls, e-mail, and communication on paper are all extremely useful.

## APPRECIATE

When a district has an effective mentor program, it is because caring and concerned individuals have contributed to its development and success. Do not take any of those supporters for granted. Superintendents, district administrators, principals, assistant principals, secretaries, department heads, directors, and business partners all play important roles in the operations of the mentor program. Simple acknowledgments can be effective ways to let individuals know their contributions are appreciated. Every contribution is important.

Without mentors, there is no mentor program—but some mentors are more effective than others. To be effective, the mentor must be willing to accept the policies and procedures established by the program; therefore, mentors should go through some basic mentor training. Mentors should possess several of the qualifications suggested in Chapter 2, "The Beginning of a Mentor Program." Most principals are willing to accept these responsibilities when they are asked to support a new principal (and they usually support the program without giving much thought to compensation). A school district should recognize the time commitment and dedication that mentors have invested in new principals and in the school district. Most districts provide each mentor a stipend for sharing time and expertise. This gesture communicates a positive message from the district. Normally, the stipend is small, but the message sent is important.

Business partners can be important assets to a mentor program that is probably operating on a small budget. When approached with a clear purpose, business partners may help fill the void in resources and funds for support of mentoring activities that district funds might not be able to provide. Business partners may contribute support for publications, congratulatory memorabilia, small appreciation gifts, and refreshments for training and in-service opportunities. Whatever the need, if it can be justified, business partners usually will provide support.

Encouraging people to give time, skills, expertise, and resources can be an art. By making these significant contacts, a mentor program can prosper. Part is tangible, and part is intangible. If applied to the program effectively, both parts create a sense of pride and involvement that enhances the vision of the school, district, and community.

The progressive levels of recognition and appreciation list (Exhibit 5A) might be used as a gauge for determining a level of recognition one might wish to express. The mentor stipend is one of several creative ways that the program and district can express appreciation.

**Exhibit 5A**    Progressive Levels of Recognition and Appreciation

- A spoken thank you
- A written thank you
- A tangible item, i.e., flowers, candy, small gift
- Being honored or recognized within a small group
- Being honored or recognized within a large group
- Being honored or recognized in a publication
- Being honored or recognized with a certificate, plaque, or trophy
- Being honored or recognized with a certificate, plaque, or trophy at a formal event
- Being awarded compensation: time off, stipend, raise, or promotion

## THE MORALE FACTOR

Morale may be directly correlated with stress and burnout. Low morale can increase levels of both stress and burnout. It is disheartening to hear comments from principals such as, "No one cares about what I do right, but let me do one thing wrong and I never hear the end of it," "I don't think anyone appreciates the effort I put in at my school," or "I didn't take this job for the money, but it would be nice if someone cared." Comments like these leave little doubt about why there is a principal shortage approaching crisis proportions. We must champion strategies to improve morale.

By incorporating simple enhancements into operations, a district can help new principals feel better about their roles and can promote confidence and self-worth. When it is a district's intent to recruit and retain principals, supporting, encouraging, complimenting, and praising may help improve morale and minimize the shortage.

The following scenarios will help illustrate the effectiveness of recognition and appreciation.

## SCENARIOS: EXTRA SUPPORT FOR SUPPORTERS

### Donna

Donna was a central office receptionist who expressed interest in the mentor program. After several brief conversations, she was presented with a single rose and a card of appreciation for her interest in the mentor program.

After observing the large amount of mail being processed for the mentor program, Donna offered to help address and stuff envelopes for mailings because she wanted to contribute to the program, and because she had time between other office responsibilities. Donna received several roses and thank-you notes over the next three years as well as a Certificate of Appreciation, which she proudly hung in her work area.

### Mary

Mary, secretary to the mentor program's control agent, was assigned the responsibility of managing the program cost accounts. She provided basic assistance such as preparing time sheets, compiling mileage reimbursement requests, and ordering supplies. On several occasions, the mentor program expressed appreciation for her support. The coordinator presented Mary with cards of appreciation and flowers during Administrative Professionals' Week and a gift certificate during the holidays. When the mentor handbook was developed, Mary offered to bind the handbooks during slow periods in the office. Mary bound four hundred and fifty handbooks over a two-week period and continued voluntarily to bind the handbooks for several years until the district printing department took over the task. Mary continued to receive appreciation on a personal level and in mentor newsletters and was invited to attend a mentor luncheon where she was recognized for her support of the program. She, too, received a Certificate of Appreciation at the end of each year, as well as a plaque recognizing her many years of support.

### District Support

Through the years, Albuquerque Public Schools (APS) superintendents provided strong support for the mentor program and took time to attend several scheduled activities. They personally signed more than seventy Certificates of Appreciation each year. Their support, as well as that of the other level superintendents, has been recognized with various levels of appreciation.

### Business Partners

Business partners have provided funds for the mentor activities throughout the years. These partners work very closely with the school community and are aware of the significance of a principal mentor program. They have been very generous and supportive, and their support has been appreciated. Business partners receive recognition in the mentor handbook, newsletters, and at sponsored events, and they have received plaques and Certificates of Appreciation at the end of each year.

### Scenario Conclusions

A good rule of thumb is never to take anyone for granted. Most people want to feel good about themselves and will respond to praise and acts of appreciation in a positive way and even by doing more. Finding ways to promote positive attitudes and self-esteem are effective ways to enrich the support you receive, whether it is for a mentor program or in your family environment. There is a difference between doing a job and doing a job well. The difference can often be stimulated by how the person doing the job is perceived and treated.

> Appreciation promotes motivation, enthusiasm, and self-esteem; lack of appreciation, ridicule, and criticism promote very little.
>
> —CJW

### KEY POINTS

1. Most people will respond in positive ways when they feel valued and appreciated.

2. If the goal is to maintain a mentor program that will provide lasting support for beginning principals, many of the components mentioned should become best practices.

3. Support systems can be a most effective source for counteracting stress and burnout.

## RECOMMENDED READINGS

Young, P., Sheets, J., & Knight, D. (2005). *Mentoring principals: Framework, agendas, tips, and case stories for mentors and mentees.* Thousand Oaks, CA: Corwin Press.

Zachary, L. J. (2005). *Creating a mentoring culture: The organizational guide.* San Francisco: Jossey-Bass.

# Applying the     **6**
# Mentoring Concept to
# Small School Districts

**W**hat about small, rural, or isolated communities? What about charter schools? Can a safe, simple, and supportive mentoring philosophy succeed in areas where there are limited resources or few schools, or where schools are geographically isolated? It is possible for small communities surrounding rural independent school districts and districts covering vast areas to combine their resources for the benefit of the new principals in the area. If there is a key formula for success, it is this: "Keep it simple."

The safe, simple, and supportive philosophy can be used in all these situations. Simplicity will help interested staff identify commonalities within each district or school that could be the foundation for mentor program development. The fundamental purpose should be to produce a base of experienced principals who will be willing to serve as mentors for beginning principals within a given area (although schools may be separated by long distances) and to provide a system that will unite a mentor and mentee.

Charter schools are unique, with their own challenges. Because they are sometimes perceived as being a threat to the public school system, they may receive less support from other schools in their area. However, charter schools remain part of a district educational structure. When appropriate, they should be included in the district support system, although their internal educational structure may be somewhat different. If there are several charter schools within a given area, these schools, because of their autonomy, may want to consider developing a support system independent of the school district initiative. The same strategies may be used in program development.

New Mexico is a rural educational community. Only seven of eighty-nine New Mexico districts have two or more high schools. The

Albuquerque Public Schools (APS) district, which has twelve high schools, is the twenty-seventh largest metropolitan district in the nation. Gallup-McKinley County Schools District has the unique distinction of being one of the largest geographical districts in the nation. With almost five thousand square miles, it is almost as large as Connecticut. The Gallup-McKinley County Schools District has eight high schools. The most distant elementary school is more than one hundred miles from the district office, and several schools are more than fifty miles from the district office. There are many similar situations like this throughout the United States. The need for mentor support for new administrators may be critical and essential in these areas. It is important to examine the need for support for new administrators in isolated areas.

Attending public school in rural Oklahoma, working in one of the largest rural and geographical school districts in the nation, and serving as a consultant for a rural region in Northern New Mexico helped create my awareness that small and rural schools have a uniqueness that must be experienced to appreciate. The uniqueness comes in the individuality of each community: "not only are rural schools different from urban and suburban schools—they also differ markedly from one another. Because each rural situation is unique, there can be no one-size-fits-all approach to either rural education or to the preparation of leaders for rural schools" (Institute for Educational Leadership [IEL], 2005, 1).

Because of these sometimes extreme differences in school districts, maintaining the simplicity of mentor support is critical to the success of a formal principal mentor program. The individuality of each district involved can become an issue if this simplicity is not maintained. Both human and material resources can vary greatly between neighboring districts; the local tax base also impacts those resources. For example, a small rural district may operate with a superintendent and possibly one or two principals. Neighboring towns or communities may be large enough to have one or two high schools and different schools that feed in to each high school. In a situation such as this, the district could be large enough to have a superintendent and other centrally located staff, in addition to several principals and assistant principals. Some communities could readily develop a mentoring program to meet their needs, but outlying schools with one superintendent or one principal may have fewer resources.

All districts, no matter their size, must contend with national issues such as the mandates of *No Child Left Behind*. What larger districts may take for granted in services and resources might be luxuries in outlying areas. Unless the larger districts are willing to consider isolated and rural programs to be part of the larger community, it will continue to be a constant struggle for smaller school districts to acquire resources and mentor support while being held to the same academic standards.

A support system that could benefit a larger district or rural district will take collaborative thought and deliberate planning. The initial planning and development could be time consuming, but, once the program is established, an organized program should be profitable to both new and experienced administrators. It is imperative to commit resources, to communicate, and to cooperate if the endeavor is to succeed. The following suggestions might be helpful in planning and implementing a basic support system for beginning principals who are cut off or isolated from areas that are more populous.

## ORGANIZE A STUDY COMMITTEE

Someone must start the process. This could be an individual principal, a group of principals, a district administrator, or any educator. That person should discuss the mentoring concept with the superintendent and others and solicit district involvement as early as possible in the process. Since superintendents in smaller districts are directly involved in most aspects of the decision-making process, their involvement is critical.

The principal mentoring program could be placed on district agendas for open discussion. If agreement can be reached on the need, a study committee could explore the possibilities. Superintendents or a designated coordinator could assign principals or other personnel to represent their districts. Other possible members could be from human resources, finance, or other agencies. Community leaders can be included, as could a superintendent or other educators.

Once the committee has been established, a chair should be identified to ensure that the process is coordinated and responsibilities assigned. Agreement should be reached on a meeting schedule and a timeline so dates can be placed on members' calendars. It is significant for all participants to commit to the planning process. Rotating meeting locations also helps committee members increase their knowledge of the districts. (School districts may be able to provide mileage reimbursement for committee members.)

## PURPOSE OF THE STUDY COMMITTEE

The purpose of the study committee is to review and assess the possibility of developing a principal mentor program that would provide support for new principals within a given geographical area or school district. The objective may focus on the research and development that would justify the need.

The following suggestions may help achieve a committee's objectives:

- Devote the first meeting to a committee discussion of each district's or school's concerns and how a mentor program may have value to a beginning principal in each district or school.
- Once the committee agrees on the objective, it needs to develop a preliminary vision and mission statement that would help provide direction and purpose for the project. (Reviewing the section on "Vision and Mission Statements" in Chapter 3, "A Work in Process," might help provide direction.)
- Researching data and information will be helpful in justifying the importance of the program. Recommended readings in this handbook provide insight on mentoring that might be useful in establishing purpose and need. Surveys or questionnaires may be used to identify support and resources for the program. (The surveys or questionnaires should be designed to address the specific issues related to the region being considered.)
- Determine if a mentor program is feasible.
- As research and justification are developed, include a program description that may include areas such as guidelines, processes, coordinator job descriptions, mentor job descriptions, and other areas unique to the community. (Again, the examples in Chapter 3, "A Work in Process," might be useful.) It is important to consider who will coordinate the program once it is established. A region ordinarily will not have more than five or six new principals per year, so the position need not be full time. One option might be to consider a retired administrator who lives in the region. Alternatively, the position could be assigned to a district staff member. Both options should be minimal in cost. The responsibilities become more time consuming only when too many activities are incorporated into the basic program.
- It does not take large amounts of money to operate a basic mentor program. The two main expenses are usually compensation for the coordinator and mentor stipends. The committee should develop a budget and submit it to the superintendents. Let the superintendents determine how program expenses might be shared. The superintendents (or designees) may determine how the distribution will be made, or if expenses should be divided equally or prorated based on the number of schools in each district. Compensation for the coordinator and the mentors must be addressed; paying them as consultants may work in some districts. Compensation for the mentor should come from the

district being served, and the mentor stipend amount should be agreed on by the superintendents. Coordinator compensation might be based on the number of new principals identified in the region.

- Once the program has been developed and approved, the coordinator should be identified, after which he or she should begin working with the committee. Next, the mentor identification process begins. The coordinator may obtain all the names, business phone numbers, e-mail addresses, and number of years of experience of all principals in each district from the identified region. (District offices will have this information.) A survey should be sent to every principal in the region with a letter explaining the purpose for the survey. (E-mail often simplifies this process.) Personal or professional information such as name, address, phone number, e-mail address, administrative position, school location, and years of educational experience (as teacher or principal or both) should be gathered in the survey. This survey can be the start of a mentor base for the area. After this information is obtained, a mentor application should be developed and sent to all experienced principals to determine specific mentor profiles and the willingness of the principal to participate in the program. (See Exhibit 8A in Chapter 8, which is a sample mentor application to address some of the basic information needed for mentor applicants.)

- Mentor applications should be compiled based on location, experience, strengths, and willingness to support the program. Most mentor programs use four or five years of experience as a baseline for establishing a mentoring position. This baseline may have to be adjusted depending on the availability of potential mentors. (Request that all applications be returned by a specific date, whether or not the recipient is interested in being a mentor.) After the mentor list is compiled, let each superintendent review the list of mentors from his or her district. There may be concerns about some individuals as mentors, so it is important to maintain limited confidentially of the approved list. No positive purpose will be served by announcing who was or was not accepted. Only the coordinator, committee, and superintendents need to have access to the list at this point.

- The new principal (mentee) might suggest names of potential mentors. If one of those recommendations is on the list, the mentor preference may be assigned. If a new principal suggests a principal who is not on the list, the coordinator should inform the new principal that the choice is not available at this time and that the mentee should consider other mentor candidates from the approved list. Giving the mentee a voice in the selection process helps provide a level of trust and confidence. If the mentee does not know any of the potential mentors, the coordinator can suggest principals from the approved list. This maintains the integrity of the process and holds true to the concept of the program being safe, simple, and supportive.

- Several criteria should be considered when assigning mentors, the most important of which is compatibility. If trust and confidence cannot be established, chances are that little productive communication will occur. Other considerations should be a mentor's areas of strength or expertise, school proximity, and administrative style. Although level-to-level assignments (such as elementary to elementary) might be advantageous, research indicates having matches made level to level has no impact on the success of a mentor relationship (Daresh, 2001, p. 59; Bloom, Castagna, Moir, & Warren, 2005, p. 111). Human resource limitations or distance might dictate the need to cross levels to ensure an effective mentor relationship.

- Once the list has been established, the coordinator responsible for assigning mentors will be able to assist a superintendent's request for mentor support for a new principal. The coordinator would begin the process by contacting the new principal who has been identified by a superintendent or human resources department. The proximity of the coordinator to the new principal may determine the practicality of a face-to-face meeting or if other means of communication should be considered. After consulting with the mentee and establishing support and a potential mentor, the coordinator would contact the selected mentor to ensure he or she will accept the mentoring opportunity. If the opportunity is accepted, the coordinator would confer with the mentor and encourage that educator to contact the mentee as soon as possible. Technology-based communication in isolated areas will suffice but, if possible, the first contact should be in person. "Through a trial-and-error method, it was discovered that the technology-based tools work best if introduced after trust has been built through face-to-face sessions" (IEL, 2005, p. 6).

When distance is a problem, an initial contact might be encouraged at a meeting both will be attending. If the mentor and mentee know one another, it can simplify the first contact, which can then be handled successfully by phone or e-mail. During the initial contact, the mentor and mentee should establish their methods of communication and the frequency of contacts, areas of support, and other criteria recommended within the program guidelines.

- For isolated areas, communities and districts can pursue plans for implementing improved communication and support. To accomplish this vision, it may take creative coordination and computer communication technology such as interfacing, web cams, and teleconferencing with TV hook-ups for long-distance collaboration or mentoring. Dr. Vita Saavedra, Director of the Educational Leadership Internship Program in the College of Education at the University of New Mexico, Albuquerque, uses this technology to conduct online visual and synchronous oral and digital telecommunications in her work with aspiring principals. Distance appears to have no bounds for the program's ability to have individual personal contact with each of the aspiring principals on a regular basis. Through her observations, research, and best practices, Dr. Saavedra enthusiastically says that, with the support of distance technology, a sense of cohort exists equal to or even greater than face-to-face interaction. This application can be applied very successfully in rural and isolated schools. The technological investment would be time and cost effective. No longer can distance or school size be a deterrent for providing routine support for a neophyte principal. (Grants are often available to support this type of technological endeavor.)

- Once a basic mentor program has been established, assessments can be made about when and if to expand it. Mentor training should be a priority. When training is not available, resources such as those suggested in the Recommended Reading section about mentoring could be helpful. Also, in-service opportunities should be considered. At some point, the program could be expanded by applying for private or federal grants. Consider grants with caution, however, because they may require time-consuming accountability practices. Educational grant opportunities can be researched through search engines on the Internet.

In some cases, an isolated new principal might have to be so bold as to personally contact an area principal and ask the individual to be a mentor, as reflected in the following scenario.

## SCENARIO: A SIMPLE FORM OF MENTORING

Jack is a first-year principal in the Pleasant Grove Independent School District, a district with 283 students (preK–12) and one superintendent. Jack works closely with preK–5, and with the total school. He teaches a fifth-grade class in the morning and coaches high school basketball or baseball (depending on the season) the last period of the day. Jack carries out some of his principal responsibilities before and after school and from 11:30 a.m.–2:00 p.m. Responsibilities can be overwhelming for a new principal, and Jack is concerned about being isolated from administrators with similar schedules. Jack hesitates to ask what might be considered naïve (or "dumb") questions of his superintendent. Jack needed to talk to someone other than his superintendent who could relate to his issues.

Jack has met most of the area administrators at administrative meetings, but most encounters were congratulatory in nature, with the usual "If you need any help, give me a call" offer being made by several. He has only conversed with a couple for any length of time and is beginning to feel as though he were on a deserted island. Although he has teaching responsibilities, he does not feel that the teaching staff totally accepts him as part of their group. His teachers are cordial and professional but they are unable to understand his isolation. He can ask questions of or vent to his superintendent, but there is no one else to be his sounding board.

At an administrators' meeting, Jack meets Harvest, an experienced principal from a nearby rural district. Jack finally developed the courage to contact Harvest. Jack asks him if he could stop by his school for a lunch visit. A date was set and Jack arrives as scheduled. During the lunch meeting, Jack asks Harvest if he knows anything about mentoring. Harvest knows only a little about the subject. Jack tells him he has been doing some reading on the subject of mentoring administrators and shares some of the aspects of the process. Jack asks Harvest if he would be willing to advise him, share his opinions, or be available to talk to from time to time. He suggests mentoring might be the way to approach his concerns. After reviewing the mentoring concepts, Harvest says he would be happy to be Jack's informal mentor. Jack and Harvest agree to keep in touch either by phone or by e-mail on a weekly basis. They also agree to have lunch at one of their schools at least once a month. They look forward to spending time discussing issues at area meetings.

Jack tells his superintendent that Harvest is going to be his mentor. The superintendent approves the concept of mentoring and suggests Harvest keep her informed about planning sessions.

## Scenario Conclusions

Jack's situation is not unique in schools in rural America. Having people around does not mean a person has someone in whom to confide. Much like Jack, the desire to share problems and seek opinions or advice can become overwhelming. In areas where human resources are limited and complex, formal mentor programs are going to be difficult to find and would probably not even be practical. This is why those who seek mentoring are encouraged to start out simply and go slowly, basing the development on needs and resources. This chapter does not imply this will be an easy task in rural districts, nor will principals in those small districts be able to achieve what a large metropolitan district can accomplish. In some cases, much like Jack's, principals might have to fend for themselves.

## KEY POINTS

1.  Establishing a mentor program in rural and small communities can be complicated since there can be no one-size-fits-all approach.

2.  Identifying commonalties can be a starting point once the need is determined and becomes a formal (or even informal) priority.

3.  Limited human resources will always present a challenge for program development.

4.  Having a cohort to talk with, share with, or seek advice from can help minimize stress and improve morale.

5.  A mentoring concept can be the difference between a new principal's adjusting to the position or just simply giving up and leaving.

6.  Welcoming a new principal to a district or region and telling him or her to call to get help is an ineffective way to provide support. A mentor program formalizes the process.

7.  The new principal may feel more comfortable approaching a mentor if there are established guidelines and mentor compensation. While districts may emphasize administrative and management skills, mentor support needs to be provided to expand a new principal's leadership skills, knowledge, and understanding of curriculum and instruction. New administrators must be encouraged to study or share strategies that will assist them in promoting student achievement.

8.  Research the latest technological advances for conducting online visual and synchronous communications to determine what would be most effective for your district.

9.  When mentor compensation is provided, an even higher level of involvement should be expected.

10. While districts or regions can provide training in curriculum development, it may be the experienced mentor who can successfully guide the neophyte through this first year.

With a safe, simple, and supportive approach, size or unique isolation should not preclude a mentoring concept. Collaboration and cooperation within and between school districts can improve success with students and enhance new administrators' talents. Although the suggestions in this section may not be applicable to your school situation, it is important to create awareness that principals in rural areas and small communities have the availability of resources to support isolated schools and administrators. Maintaining a safe, simple, and supportive environment is even possible when schools are separated by distance. Because of the uniqueness of the small and rural schools, whatever course you take, "Keep it simple!"

## RECOMMENDED READING

Institute for Educational Leadership (IEL). (2005). Preparing leaders for rural schools: Practice and policy considerations. IEL, Washington, DC. http://www.iel.org/pubs/ruralleaders.pdf.

# The Accountability 7
# Factor

The question of accountability has been raised in discussions of the simplicity of the Albuquerque Public Schools (APS) mentor program. As indicated in Chapter 9, "Finding Time to Become an Instructional Leader," members of the advisory board made clear the need for accountability within the program, but also made clear that the process not be a complex, time-consuming issue for program participants. If accountability is expected, how will it be measured, and what are the indicators of success?

## END-OF-THE-YEAR EVALUATIONS

Every mentor and mentee in the mentor program has been asked to respond to an end-of-the-year evaluation. There has always been at least a 90 percent response rate to these evaluations. In addition, these evaluations have been overwhelmingly positive, with positive, constructive comments. The program has made several improvements suggested by the recommendations. Evaluation summaries are shared with all advisory board members and all district administrators. The evaluation summaries are published in the following year's edition of the mentor handbook.

Exhibits 7A and 7B are sample "End-of-the-Year Evaluation" forms for mentees and mentors.

## ALTERNATIVE ASSESSMENTS

### Individual Feedback

Informally, mentees and mentors are encouraged to share their feelings, positive or negative, with the coordinator or members of the advisory board. It is the coordinator's responsibility to resolve any issues that may arise. The coordinator attempts to stay in contact with all parties on an informal basis to determine when intervention is needed.

**Exhibit 7A**    Survey for Mentees

Please circle the appropriate answer.

| | | | |
|---|---|---|---|
| 1. How much have you benefited from the professional development by the ESP program? | A lot | Some | Not as much as I had hoped |
| Comments: | | | |
| 2. How much has your mentor helped you develop into a more effective leader? | A lot | Some | Not as much as I had hoped |
| Comments: | | | |
| 3. How much support has your mentor provided for you? | A lot | Some | Not as much as I had hoped |
| Comments: | | | |
| 4. How much support has the ESP coordinator provided? | A lot | Some | Not as much as I had hoped |
| Comments: | | | |
| 5. How much has the ESP program benefited you? | A lot | Some | Not as much as I had hoped |
| Comments: | | | |
| 6. Would you recommend that new principals participate in the ESP program? | Yes | No | Not sure |
| Comments: | | | |
| 7. Would you recommend that all new principals be required to participate in the ESP program? | Yes | No | Not sure |
| Comments: | | | |
| 8. Should the ESP program continue? | Yes | No | Not sure |
| Comments: | | | |
| 9. How could the ESP program be improved? | | | |
| 10. Additional comments about the program: | | | |

**Exhibit 7B**  Survey for Mentors

Please circle the appropriate answer.

| 1. How much do you think your mentee has benefited from the ESP program? | A lot | Some | Not as much as I had hoped |
|---|---|---|---|
| Comments: | | | |
| 2. How much have your leadership skills improved as a result of the program? | A lot | Some | Not as much as I had hoped |
| Comments: | | | |
| 3. How much necessary support has the ESP coordinator provided for you? | A lot | Some | Not as much as I had hoped |
| Comments: | | | |
| 4. Would you recommend that new principals participate in the ESP program? | Yes | No | Not sure |
| Comments: | | | |
| 5. Would you recommend that all new principals be required to participate in ESP? | Yes | No | Not sure |
| Comments: | | | |
| 6. Would you recommend that experienced principals participate in ESP as mentors? | Yes | No | Not sure |
| Comments: | | | |
| 7. Should the ESP program continue? | Yes | No | Not sure |
| Comments: | | | |
| 8. How do you think the ESP program compares to other APS initiatives in the past 10 years? | A lot | Some | Not as much as I had hoped |
| Comments: | | | |
| 9. How could the ESP program be improved? | | | |
| 10. Additional comments about the program: | | | |

## Anecdotal Reflections

Following are some reflections from principals who have participated in the program as mentee, mentor, or both.

> Changing job duties and assignments is sometimes a difficult task but the mentor program gave me the self-confidence and assurance I needed to make a smooth transition from assistant principal to principal. As instructional leaders in our schools, we often need others to bounce ideas off of before making decisions. Getting this input from my mentor and collaborating on issues made my first year of being a principal productive and successful. (Stephanie Fasatelli, Principal, Apache Elementary, APS, Albuquerque, NM)

> Because Nikki has more administrative experience than I, I probably grew as much, if not more, from this experience than she did. We have been able to share information and strategies about how to deal with unique situations because, even if they are similar, they are never the same. Two minds are always better than one. Both of us are also members of an administrative Collaborative Learning Community. Activities such as mentorships and CLCs help principals to not be isolated in their practice. (Grace Brown, Principal, Cibola High School, APS, Albuquerque, NM)

> Perhaps, as a new principal, it is natural to experience self-doubt. Having performed many of the tasks of an administrator as an assistant principal, I was not prepared for the psychological effect of assuming the mantle of the title "Principal." The managerial aspect of a school year suddenly became overshadowed by the responsibility of leadership, that elusive quality that each principal must master if a school community is to flourish.

> In the midst of this self doubt, a red rose arrived at my door in the hand of Carl Weingartner, coordinator of Extra Support for Principals (ESP). While the rose itself was a bright spot in my day, the rose was just a representation of the actual support structure provided by the APS Principals' Mentorship Program. The program provided a mentor of my choice (in addition to Carl), a peer group with which to share experiences, and a handbook of "everything you need to know and when you need to know it." The collegiality of the social opportunities and the professional development provided by ESP and supported by our district administrators helped replace that feeling of self-doubt with self-confidence.

> While it is realistic to expect that the first years of any administrator's career will be challenging, it is comforting to know that

'someone out there' believes that I deserve a red rose. My challenge now, is to share the *red rose* concept with my educational family. Thus will our gardens grow! (Glenda Armstrong, Principal, Bandelier Elementary School, APS, Albuquerque, NM)

Five years ago, I was thrilled to be appointed as principal at Eisenhower Middle School. The night before my first day, however, panic set in and my thoughts centered more around 'What the heck did I think I was doing?!' The ESP Mentor Program helped me survive that first year, not only giving me someone I could contact for support at a moment's notice, but also connecting me with other brand-new principals as well as their mentors. In addition, the seminars provided helped me to muddle through all those 'things' that come up when you don't know where to turn. The ESP Mentor Program is wonderful! (Debbie Hamilton, Principal, Eisenhower Middle School, APS, Albuquerque, NM)

My first year as a principal ran the full spectrum of emotions and feelings. I was excited, tired, confused, stressed, upbeat, satisfied, concerned and determined all within the same day. What I have learned, specifically from my mentor, has been balance. We are confronted with issues and situations from the minute we walk into the school. I have learned to listen and address each one of the items that is presented to me, but not to overreact or not to avoid any one of them. Another important lesson I have learned is that this job cannot be done alone. No matter how good you are, there is no way one can run a school alone. I have learned, also from my mentor, how to work with consensus and as a team. The job of a principal these days requires working with many people and doing activities in a cooperative manner. I always thought that I had to be the expert in all aspects of operating a school. This is not true. I may be an expert in some areas, but seeking the advice and recommendations of the people around you will make you a better leader . . . and a better person. Thank you—Gracias. (Manuel Hernandez-Alzaga, Principal, Collet Park Elementary, APS, Albuquerque, NM)

I am a product and a mentor of the Albuquerque principal mentor program. As I thought about the program from both angles, it occurred to me that the biggest support comes from my own metacognitive growth. As a mentee, I questioned my mentor, sought his advice, looked at issues from different sides, and then came to conclusions. As a mentor, I had to do the same thing—this time from an experienced principal's outlook. The outlooks may have changed but the important process of thinking, discussing, and re-thinking has kept me growing as a professional. That is invaluable. (Letha Oman, Principal, McCollum Elementary, APS, Albuquerque, NM)

I have participated in the program as a mentee as well as a mentor. I was an experienced administrator in two states prior to my appointment to Zuni ES as principal. Therefore, I did not need a great deal of support but our mentor program was exactly what I wanted and needed. It has the flexibility to allow my personality, skills, experience, and interests to match my mentor's, whom I picked! To this day, we are good friends and supportive of each other.

Three years later, my role changed to the role of mentor. I had the opportunity to team up with a skilled administrator who moved into a first time principal position. Once again, we were able to personalize the support system to match her strengths (which were many) and her growth areas! I continued to learn from the experience and enjoyed the camaraderie with a colleague.

This year, I am once again a mentor. My mentee has a different situation and that requires more time and effort. What I appreciate, and I'm sure the mentee does, too, is the freedom to determine what works for both of us. Again, we picked each other and therefore, we are our greatest supporters. The ease of our mentor program makes it possible! (Mary Render, Principal, Zuni Elementary, APS, Albuquerque, NM)

My mentor experience is one that is worth a million dollars! I am honored to be the mentor of one of the most inspiring and passionate leaders the APS has on board. Mrs. Loretta Huerta is the principal at Reginald Chavez where she delivers quality leadership skills to a school that respects her as a person and as an instructional leader. A strong and successful mentorship comes when the mentor and mentee begin to build a professional relationship through effective communication and constant support. One example of our partnership is including our teachers to share their expertise and best practices with each other. Eugene Field Elementary and Reginald Chavez Elementary are considered sister schools, thanks to our Principal Mentoring Program! (James Luján, Principal, Eugene Field Elementary, APS, Albuquerque, NM)

## PROGRAM EVALUATIONS

There are two in-service opportunities each year, one each semester. At the end of the in-service session, evaluations are collected, summarized, and shared with the advisory board and the superintendents. A numeric rating scale of 1 to 10 is used, and areas for comment are provided. Results for the Inservice Evaluations (Exhibit 7C) are used to improve the support program.

**Exhibit 7C**   Extra Support for Principals: Principal Mentor Program In-Service Evaluation

---

Date _____

In-service Topic _____

On a scale from 1 to 10, please rate this total in-service program:

Low *1 2 3 4 5 6 7 8 9 10* High          Rating Number: _____

I learned (relearned) _____

_____

_____

I want to know more about _____

_____

_____

I will use _____

_____

_____

General  comments _____

_____

_____

Please check one: _____ I am a mentor _____ I am a first-year principal

Name (optional) _____

---

## ESP TEN-YEAR PROGRAM ASSESSMENT (1995–2005)

The following data were collected from records covering the first ten years of the ESP mentor program. This project was an attempt to track how effective the mentor support program was in retaining principals. Results indicate that the mentor program has had a positive impact on the retention factor for principals. Following are the impact categories, with a general explanation of each.

- *Principals Still in the Principalship.* This represents principals who went through the mentor program and are still principals today. Several are still in the same principalships they held as mentees, while others have taken on assignments at different schools.
- *Retired.* Several principals have retired. Many who retired from the principalship did so to take other jobs outside of education so they could draw two salaries. Some retired from the district to move to other states and were hired as principals, or in some other capacity in the field of education. A few went into other fields.
- *Promoted Within the District.* These are individuals who have accepted other positions within the district. Some positions were upper-level administrative, while others were district-support positions.
- *Back to the Classroom.* This group of principals returned to the classroom because they felt they were not suited for the principalship or because they could make as much money as a teacher with a shorter contract or fewer responsibilities, or both.
- *Left the District.* This is the largest group of principals. This group left the district for one of a multitude of reasons. Some left because their spouses were transferred, others left because of better offers within the field of education, while a few left education for other areas or careers.
- *Demotions and Resignations.* A few were demoted to lower administrative positions by the district or were reassigned to classroom positions. None of these moves was voluntary; one was a resignation due to arrest for drug possession.
- *Deceased.* One died while serving as a principal.

Exhibits 7D and 7E indicate the stability and mobility rates of the principals who participated in the mentor program over the first ten years.

The APS district has 131 principal positions. Several schools have had more than one principal during this ten-year period. There are only ten current principals who were principals before the mentor program was implemented.

**Exhibit 7D**    Mobility Rate, 1995–2005

Of 177 new principals

- 118 are still in the principalship (66.5 percent)
- 9 have retired (5 percent)
- 11 have been promoted within the district (6 percent)
- 5 went back to the classroom by choice (3 percent)
- 29 left the district (16.5 percent)
- 4 were demoted or resigned (2 percent)
  - o 3 were **demoted** (1.5 percent)
  - o 1 **resigned** (0.5 percent)
- 1 is deceased (0.5 percent)

*Note:* Percentages were rounded off during the calculations.

**Exhibit 7E**    ESP Program Mobility Rate

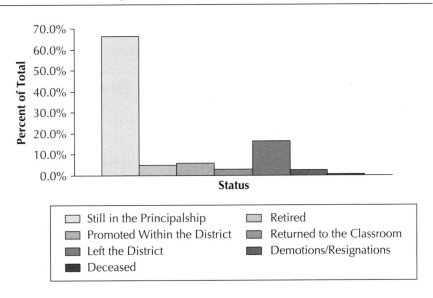

*Source:* Data compiled from ESP records covering the ten-year period from 1995 through 2005.

Of the principals who have gone through the program, 118 from the category of "still in the principalship" and 11 from the category of "promoted within the district" represent 73 percent of the positive outcomes. Four of those promotions have been to upper-level administrative positions, which could also be considered a positive indicator for the mentor support system. Therefore, we can conclude that ESP has been successful in providing an appropriate support system that has helped in the retention of a high percentage of principals for an extended time.

In her 2006 book, *Mentoring and Induction Programs That Support New Principals*, Dr. Susan Villani did a comparison study of mentor programs across the nation. Her approach was to identify program models based on specific criteria and program similarities that included funding sources and sponsorships, i.e., district and regional models, state models, professional association models, university models, and collaborative models. The APS ESP mentor program was included in her research, which provided us with an opportunity to compare the ESP program to other similar programs, as well as to programs with different goals and objectives.

Evaluation is a significant part of any successful program. It would be difficult to professionally determine the strengths or areas for improvement without an evaluative process. Some possible formative questions follow.

- How much do we want to know?
- How might we obtain the information we seek?
- How much time will be involved in the process of obtaining the information?
- Who will be impacted by the information obtained?
- How will we use the information?
- What purpose will the information serve?

By addressing these questions, we can determine how to proceed in designing the assessment tools needed to obtain the desired information. The mentor assessment process not only includes surveys and question-naires similar to the ones presented in this chapter, but also other indica-tors such as

- Principals' willingness to participate in the program
- High attendance at mentor functions
- Participants' enthusiasm
- Principals' willingness to serve and support the program
- The collegiality and bond exhibited between mentors and mentees
- Participants' feelings of being honored to be part of the process
- District administrations' participation in program functions

Combinations of both the surveys and observations are clear indica-tors of program stability.

**KEY POINTS**

1. Accountability is critical for the success of a mentor program.

2. The value of documentation and record keeping should be weighed against the benefits obtained for the principals involved.

3. All activities related to data gathering should be appropriate and timely.

4. Anecdotal records should be used when the major benefit would be to the mentor and mentee. Some studies indicate that record keeping is not an effective use of time. There are cases where some principals do not respond until a day or two before records are due to be turned in, at which point it becomes a race of checking the calendar dates and elaborating on each date briefly. Very little, if any, useful purpose benefits the mentees when measured against the time involved to maintain the records.

5. Assess the assessments; determine their benefits for the principals and program. Always factor in the element of time on every aspect of the data-gathering process.

## RECOMMENDED READINGS

Bloom, G., Castagna, C., Moir, E., & Warren, B. (2005). *Blended coaching: Skills and strategies to support principal development.* Thousand Oaks, CA: Corwin Press.

Villani, S. (2006). *Mentoring and induction programs that support new principals.* Thousand Oaks, CA: Corwin Press.

# The Art of Mentoring the Beginning Principal

**8**

**M**entoring is the process by which an individual with knowledge and skills in a field willingly shares advice and support with a beginner. Experienced principals know how challenging the principalship can be. They feel an obligation to help a new principal succeed (whether or not there is a mentoring program in place). However, willingness to help is not always enough. Even principals who have a proven record of success may not be effective mentors. "Some mentor program coordinators, as well as some administrators who are prospective mentors, do not initially see the need for the training of mentors or coaches. They believe that administrators should already have the knowledge of education and the skills needed to be effective mentors. However, good administrators do not necessarily make good coaches" (Villani, 2006, p. 19). "Research has shown that good administrative mentors must be good principals but that good principals do not always serve as good mentors" (Daresh, 2001, p. 36).

Although some seem to have the gift for mentoring, many do not become truly proficient mentors until they have at least some basic training in the art of mentoring. A district program should support mentoring by providing its experienced principals with some basic mentor training based on research and best practices. Conflicts can often arise with the question, "How much is enough?" Some programs see the need to provide continuous training on a regular basis. Often, this mentoring concept is tied to some research-based program or grant. Principals are willing to devote some time to the mentor training process, but most are not interested in obtaining a hypothetical degree in mentoring. Sometimes the term "overkill" is overheard if mentors are continually called on to participate in mentor-training activities. Therefore, a program must carefully plan and organize only essential training sessions.

## CONCEPTS FOR EFFECTIVE MENTORING

There are identifiable attributes an effective mentor should possess. A successful mentor will have many, but probably not all, of them. These attributes are grouped into specific concepts that can be applied to successful mentoring. Attributes alone do not guarantee a successful experience. When we look for the strengths in a prospective mentor, however, certain concepts become significant:

### Concept 1

- Mentors are committed to the process of mentoring.

### Concept 2

- Mentors are effective listeners.
- Mentors possess sound communication skills.
- Mentors have developed strong problem-solving skills and sound judgment.

### Concept 3

- Mentors often are visionaries.
- Mentors are creative problem solvers.
- Mentors maintain confidentiality.
- Mentors are flexible in thinking and action.

### Concept 4

- Mentors are willing to share knowledge.
- Mentors are experienced principals.

### Concept 5

- Mentors know how to ask thought-provoking questions.
- Mentors are good time managers.
- Mentors are risk takers.

### Concept 6

- Mentors are aware of community needs and expectations.
- Mentors are proud of their roles as principals.
- Mentors are able to support as well as to lead.
- Mentors are able to "back off" when necessary.

### Concept 7

- Mentors encourage mentees.
- Mentors maintain a low profile when working with mentees.
- Mentors keep their own egos in check.

### Concept 8

- Mentors have a positive outlook toward their roles as a principal and as a mentor.
- Mentors commit the time needed to effectively support their mentees.
- Mentors are willing to validate and celebrate mentee successes.

### Concept 9

- Mentors make a difference.

## ESTABLISHING THE MENTOR POOL

A pool of mentors must be available as new principals are appointed. The success of the mentor program will be tied directly to the quality of mentors. A great deal of thought must be given to the selection and preparation of mentors. Questions or concerns that need to be considered when establishing the mentor pool are the following:

1. How large is the base from which a mentor pool can be identified?

2. Should smaller districts team with other districts within a general proximity to establish a more effective mentor pool?

3. Should a mentor work with more than one mentee?

4. What will be the selection process for determining mentors?

5. Who will select the mentors, and who will match mentors with mentees?

6. Should all experienced principals be surveyed to determine the level of interest in the program, or will mentors be actively recruited?

7. Should an interview process be utilized to select mentors? If so, who should serve on the interview panel?

8. How much experience determines if a principal might be considered for a mentoring position?

9. What questions should be on a mentor application?

Most districts begin the process of developing a pool of mentors by surveying principals to determine support and interest in the mentor program development. With positive results, the next step is to develop an application for mentorship. (Exhibit 8A is a sample mentor application that includes some of the basic information needed for mentor applicants.

Other questions should be added to address specific information desired by an individual program or school district.) After applications have been made, a follow-up response form may be sent out to all who applied. This form would ask for more detailed responses useful in finalizing the mentor list and planning the preparation process.

There are several options to consider while establishing a mentor pool. The following are options that have been implemented in programs with variations and different degrees of success.

*Total Inclusion.* Because of limited human resources in small or rural school districts, it is often difficult to have a large mentor pool. To capitalize on available resources, everyone considered an "experienced" principal might be invited to participate. (Selection of mentor candidates may require a dose of reality. It might be essential to consolidate resources of several small districts in a given area to achieve the objective. In addition, rural districts may need to develop plans that might include on-line discussions with a district mentor.)

*Selection by Superintendent.* All district principals with four or five years' experience are identified, and a list of their names is given to the superintendent or designee. The superintendent scrutinizes the list and eliminates any principals considered ineligible; those who have been approved remain on the list. New principals may be given the opportunity to select a mentor from the approved list.

The positive side to this process of selection by a superintendent (or designee) is that the district-level administration is aware of the issues a specific principal may be dealing with in a given year. For either personal or professional reasons, the district administration may feel a principal might not be appropriate for a mentoring assignment during a specific year. (If the issues are resolved, that principal might be returned to the list.) Although rare, there have been occasions when decisions on who may or may not be a mentor are based on political or personality issues. Sometimes competent applicants may not be considered because a personal, professional, or political conflict exists between them and an administrator.

*Selection by Committee.* Committee selection appears to be the most popular method for establishing a mentor pool. Potential mentors are invited to apply, after which a selection committee composed of program representatives reviews and evaluates the applications. Some districts incorporate an applicant interview in this process, also. A point system may be the determining factor. Every applicant achieving at least a basic score is placed in the mentor pool. Some programs allow new principals to review the final list and make a recommendation about their selection of prospective mentors.

**Exhibit 8A**   Mentor Application

Name_____ School_____

Address_____ City_____ State_____ Zip _____

E-mail address_____ Phone #_____ Cell #_____

At what grade levels are you administratively certified? _____

How many years of experience do you have in the principalship? _____

At what levels? _____

What are your areas of expertise? _____

Have you ever participated in a mentoring program before? (yes or no) _____

If yes, where and when? _____

_____

Are you willing to devote the time to mentor a new principal, to include attendance at attend training sessions and in-service opportunities? (yes or no) _____

What would be your major concern about participating in a mentor program? _____

_____

_____

Would you expect compensation for your participation in the program mentor? (yes or no) _____

Briefly describe the concept of mentoring as you perceive it: _____

_____

_____

Signature_____ Date _____

Some programs have a get-acquainted activity, often a social event, where potential mentors and mentees come together as a group to meet as well as to identify and discuss philosophical similarities. Mentors and mentees offer suggestions to the coordinator, who makes matches based on compatibility. Mentors and mentees may know each other from previous relationships, and there may be a level of trust and respect that already exists, which is important in any relationship. Mentor-mentee matching is a critical area of program development.

A word of caution. To retain the philosophy of the safe, simple, and supportive concept, a conscious effort must be made to protect the integrity of each potential mentor. It should be a priority to create a safe process for everyone. Principals may feel a sense of rejection if they are not considered as potential mentors. One way to address this issue is not to disclose the mentor list to the general principal population, no matter which selection process is used. There is no justification for publicizing the list. Confidentiality should be honored by all involved in this process.

A simple way to address the issue is for only the district-level administrators, selection committee, or the coordinator, or a combination of these, to have knowledge of the approved list. Often the mentee will suggest a mentor without having seen the approved list. If the recommended mentor is on the list, the process can move forward without the mentee reviewing the list. If the mentee is unable to suggest a mentor, the coordinator gives the new principal the opportunity to review the mentors from the appropriate listings. In some cases, the coordinator will be able to recommend names from the approved list without revealing the total list. After a selection has been made, the appointment is announced. (Note that the mentee has a voice in the selection.) In the twelve years of the Albuquerque Public Schools (APS) mentor program, there have been only three occasions when a principal learned that he or she was not on the approved list and had not been approved as a mentor. It is critical to develop a process that will maintain the integrity of the safe, simple, and supportive concept for everyone.

## SUGGESTIONS FOR MENTORS WORKING WITH MENTEES

The suggestions for mentors working with mentees are recommendations compiled using research and collaboration with several school districts across the nation. The suggestions have been shared with other publications and websites, including the George Lucas Educational Foundation and Villani 2006, pp. 281–282. These recommendations can be helpful in establishing a positive rapport in the mentoring relationship.

1. *Be thoughtful in your approach.* When accepting the responsibility as a mentor, approach the mentee in a low-key manner. The first contact is very important. The experienced principal could be intimidating to the neophyte unless there is a caring, encouraging, and supportive relationship from the beginning.

2. *Always be positive and supportive.* The ability of the neophyte administrator to grow is dependent on self-esteem. That quality is not at risk when the mentee asks for advice, but it might be threatened by direct, thoughtless, or unsolicited advice. If the mentor really has concerns about a practice, asking questions may reveal the thinking behind the question. Sometimes a desire to "suggest" meets mentor needs more than those of the mentee.

3. *Celebrate the appointment.* Appointment to a position as a principal for the first time is an earned and exciting honor. Most new principals will be pleased and proud of the mentor's interest in their new appointment. A congratulatory card or a small gift of remembrance could be a good way to start off that first meeting. Words of encouragement from a mentor mean a great deal!

4. *Let the mentee determine how much support you can be.* Success as a mentor is dependent on the new principal's readiness and openness for learning. Watch the timing: if you offer advice too quickly, it may not be understood by the mentee. (Offer an idea once or twice. More than that and repetition becomes uncomfortable. Wait until the mentee expresses need for guidance, unless perceived issues are obvious.)

5. *Be willing to be patient.* You could make mistakes of timing or approach even though your ideas may be very good. Be open about asking for feedback from the mentee should that happen. Avoid being pushy. Lead by questioning.

6. *Don't accept ownership of mentee problems.* Your role is to advise and support. The mentee must always maintain ownership and responsibility for the outcomes.

7. *Avoid taking rejection of ideas personally.* Often rejection relates to readiness to learn and is a valuable clue to the mentee's stage of development.

8. *Continually reinforce the confidential nature of the relationship.* Thank your mentee for any confidence and for personal sharing. These are signs of a deepening and trusting relationship.

9. *Recognize the need for time outside of school.* Plan some rapport-building activities and allow for the mentee's other areas of life. Avoid overdosing on help.

10. *Be there for them.* Assure the mentee that your main objective is to be there for support, not to run the mentee's school.

11. *Collaborate with other mentoring teams.* Mentoring teams often work in the same feeder or school cluster. This would be an excellent opportunity for two or more mentoring teams to meet on occasion to share ideas about district goals and objectives, issues, and successes.

12. *Mentors gain from the experience.* As a mentor, you as well as the mentee can look forward to a positive learning experience. A new principal comes to the position with creativity and enthusiasm. Mentors may gain as much from the experience as does the mentee.

13. *Plan ahead so you are available during busy times.* Busy times for both mentee and mentor may come at the same time. Get your work coordinated ahead of time so you can collaborate when the opportunity or need arises. Effective time management is important.

14. *Offer to support district administrator or evaluator's efforts with the mentee.* In doing so, be careful not to assume the responsibilities that belong to the evaluator. The mentor program should not be part of any district evaluation process. Mentors support, and supervisors evaluate! Even the perception that the line between support and evaluation has been crossed can be inhibiting to mentees. Just let the administrator know the discussion makes you uncomfortable and suggest a meeting with the mentee present.

15. *Motivate mentees to think for themselves.* Use questions to promote higher-level thinking and to reveal the underlying reasons for decisions. Questions that have purpose and direction will motivate the mentee to evaluate possible outcomes. Take time to discuss these reasons or outcomes.

16. *Plan ways to spend time together.* Plan a "lunch getaway" or formal or spontaneous joint work sessions. These opportunities allow greater sharing and trust building.

## MENTORING VERSUS COACHING

There are many definitions of the terms "mentoring" and "coaching." Lois Zachary (2000) reflects, "Coaching and mentoring frequently get confused. As each construct has evolved over time, each has gotten increasingly harder to differentiate. Coaching is always a part of mentoring, but coaching does not always involve mentoring" (pp. 73–74). Bloom et al. (2005) write, "Coaching is not mentoring, although effective mentors use coaching skills and strategies. The terms coach and mentor are some-times used interchangeably. For the purpose of our work, however, we define a mentor as an organizational insider who is a senior expert and sup-ports a novice. A coach is typically from outside the organization and is not necessarily senior—in age or depth of related professional experiences—to the coachee" (pp. 9–10). Bruce Barnett (1987) refers to the coaching process as "peer-assisted leadership" (p. 275). As you review these and other writings, it is almost possible to interchange terminology and derive the same conclusion: to provide expert support and guidance for an inex-perienced leader. Obviously, there are several approaches to the process. It would be best to assess program needs and objectives and select an option that might include recommendations from several authors. The value is in the context, not in the semantics.

Throughout the years of the Albuquerque mentor program, experience and research have been shared with several school districts, state departments of education, and individuals. Because of this shared knowledge, the program has grown and developed into a nationally recognized mentor program for first-year principals, principals changing levels, and experienced principals new to the district. In growing from a fledgling mentor program to a highly structured support system, one notable issue surfaced frequently. "Hidden agendas" play a critical role in defining the difference between mentoring and coaching. The terms "mentoring" and "coaching" seemed to be used synonymously; this issue began to create a problem as the Albuquerque mentor program grew. The program's basic philosophy has been to provide a safe, simple, and supportive system for new principals. It was felt that "mentoring" should provide that environment, while "coaching" could have a more threatening or intimidating effect. Therefore, the program strives to clarify and emphasize the difference between mentoring and coaching.

A mentor advisory board should be committed to providing an environ-ment in which a principal could pursue questions, issues, concerns, and frustrations with an experienced peer whose sole purpose is to provide support, advice, and direction. The mentor must not bring to the program a personal agenda that might interfere with the concept of a safe environment.

## A COACHING CONCEPT

Although coaching is an excellent process used to provide growth and enrichment, it does not always provide the safe and confidential environ-ment a mentoring program offers. For instance, a basketball coach can provide instruction, advice, direction, and wisdom to a player, but the coach's agenda would be different from the mentor's agenda. A coach must win games. If the player does not learn or develop to the satisfaction of the coach, there can be consequences (less playing time, being benched, or being cut from the team). Although the player wants to achieve or exceed the coach's expectations, the coach controls the situation and determines, to a major degree, the success of the player.

In the same vein, the supervising district administrator can have the same control over a new principal—or over any principal, for that matter. With coaching, the supervisor must see improvement or a higher level of success for the improvement of a school and district. The supervisor can provide support through experienced personnel who have expertise in the areas of concern; other support and resources can be utilized as well. Through the supervisor's evaluations, outcome goals can be determined. Rewards or consequences can be based on those evaluations.

Coaching has a very distinct place in the growth and development of a principal, but it is not designed to provide the level of trust, confidence, and freedom that mentoring provides. In some cases, a new principal could use both a mentor and a coach to develop into a master principal. In mentoring, the growth and development is determined between the new principal and the mentor.

A mentor should not be part of the evaluation process. The mentor should neither pose any threat to the mentee nor represent any kind of consequence. The mentor's objective is to provide a climate of trust that permits the mentee to feel safe in risking a new perspective or behavior. The mentoring objective is to maintain safe, free, and open dialogue between the new principal and the mentor. District administrators and supervisors should not play a direct role in the mentoring program.

## SIMPLICITY

The safe, simple, and supportive program has never included dissecting the mentoring process and developing graphs, charts, surveys, and questionnaires to analyze the process. From the beginning, the program objective has been to provide a support system for beginning principals. The program has always intended to avoid time-consuming tasks that diminish the ability of the mentor to interact personally with the mentee. Some might criticize the simplicity of the program, but that criticism should be tempered by observation of the success of the objective. A survey of principals and assistant principals expressed strong feeling that first-year principals can experience more success if they have supportive, low-key mentor relationships. After twelve years and support of more than 210 first-year principals, surveys appear to bear out this philosophy.

This process of mentoring was designed not to place stress or increased demands on the new principal. It minimizes the time both the mentor and mentee would be taken away from their schools. The responsibility of the new principal is to determine the level of need. It is incumbent on the mentee to make known the desired level of mentor support that he or she finds comfortable. Communication is an important key in this relationship.

## LEVEL-TO-LEVEL MENTORING

The district coordinator will assist the new principal in selecting a mentor. A mentor should be a qualified experienced principal from the designated mentor pool. It is recommended, but not required, that the mentor be from the same district level of the appointment (high school–high school, middle school–middle school, elementary–elementary) Research, however, shows that the effectiveness of both mentor and mentee being from the same level is not supported. As John Daresh (2001) puts it, "Although it might be true many technical parts of the administration of secondary schools differ from those of the elementary school, the foundations of school leadership, as defined by much of the literature dealing with effective leaders remain the same in elementary, middle, senior high, or even post-secondary" (p. 59). The mentor advisory board felt it would be difficult for a mentor from the elementary level to support a new high school principal on how to devise a class schedule or deal with athletic issues. Therefore, it is the program's position that first consideration will be given to level-to-level matches.

## COMMUNICATE, COMMUNICATE, COMMUNICATE

After consulting and discussing potential mentors from the approved mentor list with the mentee, a selection is made. The coordinator will contact the potential mentor to offer the opportunity to become a mentor. If accepted, an appointment is made to discuss responsibilities and mentor guidelines. The mentor will be encouraged to contact the mentee and set up a planning session. Each mentor-mentee team will plan objectives and goals. Areas of focus and a regular schedule for communicating should be discussed at this first meeting.

Communication is a two-way street; both must take seriously the responsibility to maintain open lines of communication. Contact should be made at least every other week. If the mentor has not heard from the mentee, the mentor should take the opportunity to call or visit just to see how things are going. Experience shows that a minimum of three hours monthly should be devoted to communication or interaction to create an effective support system for the mentee. Quick phone calls may provide support in some cases, but experience has shown that effective communication is the single most important part of the program.

After initial meetings, the role of the program coordinator becomes secondary. The coordinator will continue to communicate as needed with mentees and mentors by personal memos, e-mail, newsletters, phone, or other electronic means. Also, it is the coordinator's responsibility to provide training, orientation, and professional development opportunities for all new principals and their mentors throughout the year.

Simply stated, the Albuquerque program is one of support for a first-year principal. The district provides a mentor for each new principal. Part of that district support is in the form of a stipend for each mentor. How much support the novice principal needs and wants to access is up to the individual. Needs will vary from person to person, but the district encourages the mentor to take their mentoring responsibility seriously. The mentees can expect a support system that will meet their needs throughout that critical first year as a principal.

The principalship can be an isolated, demanding, and stressful responsibility. If the mentor program can assist a new principal with a positive beginning, the investment made is worthwhile. The benefits to the district, to the principalship, to the schools, and to their community will be great, but the ones who will benefit the most will be the students served.

## SCENARIO: A MENTOR'S WISDOM

This scenario is based on an actual situation and demonstrates how a skillful mentor can support and advise a mentee who is dealing with a frustrating problem. Several of the mentor attributes listed in this chapter were utilized while resolving this issue.

Leroy has been a middle school principal for 14 years and is the mentor for Cynthia, who has been a middle school principal for seven months. Cynthia contacted Leroy and asked for his help and advice on a frustrating school situation. Cynthia showed Leroy to one of the girls' restrooms with a large mirror plastered with "lipstick kisses." Leroy began by asking questions to help her with the issue, which was ongoing and time consuming, not necessarily major. He pursued his line of questioning to help her consider her options. She felt that the process should not be time consuming. She said she did not want to make a big deal out of the situation but she needed to get it stopped. She was unable to come up with a simple solution.

Leroy offered a suggestion that he felt would work for him, but he cautioned Cynthia that what would work for him might not be as effective for her. Leroy suggested an elaborate plan involving his custodian. He said if it were his problem, he would ask his custodian to meet him in the girls' restroom at the end of the next day. He would ask his custodian to clean all the sinks and commodes with disinfectant water and a sponge. Then, Leroy would tell his custodian to clean the mirror with the same sponge he used to clean the commodes.

To put the plan into action, Leroy told Cynthia he would call in some of the suspected offenders to his office a few minutes before the restroom cleaning. He indicated he would discuss the lipstick problem with the girls and explain to them about the extra time it takes to clean the lipstick off the mirror. Leroy would then escort the girls to the restroom so they could observe the routine cleaning. On cue, the custodian cleaned the sinks, the commodes, and the mirror, all with the same sponge. Knowing the impact it would have on the girls, Leroy told Cynthia that, as a follow-up, he would explain the importance of the custodian's time schedule and would innocently suggest to the girls to ask their friends to help out the custodian by keeping the mirror clean.

He told Cynthia if he received any calls from parents he would share with them that everything is cleaned with water and disinfectant according to the standards of the district custodial department guidelines. If pursued, he said he would discuss the health issue of the girls putting their mouth on anything in the restroom, including the mirror.

Cynthia liked Leroy's idea and followed the plan to the letter. The day after she put the plan into action, the kisses on the mirror were cut in half; by the end of the week, the problem had been eliminated. No parents called.

## Scenario Conclusions

Often, experience will play an important role in the support of a mentee. As a beginning principal gains more experience, he or she will have many opportunities to hone reasoning and problem-solving skills. Leroy gave a good demonstration on how to solve a complex situation without expending a lot of time on it. As a mentor, he attempted to involve Cynthia in the problem solving through example. Leroy gave Cynthia the tools, but he let her have the experience of implementing the process. Cynthia learned by doing, knowing she had expert advice to guide her.

It might be helpful to review the list of mentor attributes. How many do you feel Leroy displayed during his session with Cynthia?

_____

_____

_____

_____

_____

## KEY POINTS

When designing a mentor-mentee program, one must realize the significance of each party to the program. This support system must be orchestrated effectively.

1. Being a successful principal is a prerequisite for mentoring.

2. It is important that principals realize that participation in a mentor program implies accepting fundamental strategies for a successful partnership. As Bloom and colleagues (2005) reflect, "Coaching is a complex art!" (p. 53). The same perception can apply to mentoring. Effective mentoring is truly an art!

3. Mentor training is essential. Some individuals have a natural ability to be a positive influence on a mentee, but some basic training based on research and best practices usually will be beneficial to any mentor program. Suggestions were offered for mentors to consider when supporting a new principal, creating an awareness of the importance of fundamental strategies in the mentoring process.

4. The development of a mentor pool is extremely important. Mentor recruitment can become complex, depending on the demographics of a district, size, distances, or geographic boundaries. Success can prevail in small districts if resources are pooled with other districts in the region. We must not forget the importance of keeping the mentor recruitment process safe and effective.

5. There are two basic issues concerning the mentor vs. coaching dilemma. First, "hidden agendas" kept creeping into the Albuquerque mentor program until they were identified as a component of coaching. Second, it is more important to focus on the content than on the semantics. Some experts present a strong approach with boundless research to support their recommendations and advice on the topic. For the most part, both concepts (mentoring and coaching) convey the same message: positive support. Mentors need to access the most effective concept to meet the established goals. If a particular descriptor works, use it.

## RECOMMENDED READINGS

Barnett, Bruce G. (1987). *Instructional leadership concepts, issues and controversies: Using reflection as a professional growth activity.* Columbus, OH: Allyn & Bacon.

Bloom, G., Castagna, C., Moir, E., & Warren, B. (2005). *Blended coaching: Skills and strategies to support principal development.* Thousand Oaks, CA: Corwin Press.

Daresh, J. C. (2001). *Leaders helping leaders: A practical guide to administrative mentoring.* Thousand Oaks, CA: Corwin Press.

Villani, S. (2006). *Mentoring and induction programs that support new principals.* Thousand Oaks, CA: Corwin Press.

Young, P., Sheets, J., & Knight, D. (2005). *Mentoring principals: Framework, agendas, tips, and case stories for mentors and mentees.* Thousand Oaks, CA: Corwin Press.

Zachary, L. J. (2005). *Creating a mentoring culture: The organizational guide.* San Francisco: Jossey-Bass.

# Finding Time to Become an Instructional Leader

# 9

When a new principal is assigned to a school, the first step is to begin assessing the new role and responsibilities. During this assessment, the new principal may conclude that the primary responsibility will center on becoming an instructional leader. Soon, though, reality may set in rather abruptly. New administrators quickly will be introduced to the managerial aspect of the principalship. The new leader might be inundated with so many operational, logistical, and personnel issues that curriculum development may not be the primary focus. Consider, for instance, the new high school principal who accepted the position and received the keys to the school on Friday. During that first weekend, his school was vandalized extensively.

In a recent conversation with a mentor, the question came up of how his elementary school mentee was doing. He recalled a conversation they had in which he asked the mentee if any thought had been given to improvement of the curriculum and test scores. The mentee's response was, "I haven't had time to give it much thought just yet. I've been too busy trying to find a bucket and a mop so I could clean the cafeteria because I haven't had a custodian for the past three days." Most experienced principals can relate to this beleaguered principal's situation. Planned developments are often deferred because of other pressing issues that fall under the operational management. Most principals identify themselves as instructional leaders, but they often admit they have not been able to devote the desired time to the process.

Time is a precious commodity. Mentors can be helpful by questioning, promoting, and encouraging development of time-management skills. Without this mentor support, it is easy for many new principals to flounder as they attempt to achieve all their many goals in the limited time available.

## IT'S A MATTER OF TIME

The main purpose of the Albuquerque Extra Support for Principals advisory board is to ensure that a mentor program that has been designed to support actually *does* provide support. As the mentor program was developed, the advisory board reviewed mentor programs across the nation. Several programs displayed activities and demands that seriously infringed on a principal's time. The board made it clear that a principal's time was to be respected and that any mentor-mentee activities should have a productive purpose.

The advisory board believed that program accountability was important, but the evaluation and assessment process was to remain simple and not time consuming. Observations, voluntary participation, comments, and end-of-year evaluations for mentors and mentees should be indicators of the program's success or weakness. Anecdotal records were recommended only if they served a meaningful purpose to the mentoring team.

The board believed that if a mentor program were nonexistent, a new principal in need of help or advice would contact an experienced principal whom they respected and trusted, then would deal with the issue and move on to other responsibilities. To the advisory board, it appeared that the process of anecdotal records had little or no intrinsic value when compared to the time involved. One even suggested if she were a new principal and took time to write anything, it would be a thank-you note. Documentation is possibly a program justification activity rather than a procedure to provide direct benefit to the mentee and the mentor; it does not comply with the simple philosophy of the mentor program. (In situations involving special issues, concerns, or legal activities, documentation should occur as part of any principal's school responsibilities.)

## TIME-MANAGEMENT SUGGESTIONS

Time management is one of the major survival skills a successful administrator must develop to carry out duties and responsibilities; it is particularly important for a first-year principal. Frustration easily creeps in when there is not enough time in the day to complete all the necessary tasks, and frustration leads to stress. Know what is expected of you and focus on organization. Map out strategies and organize a plan of action. Be aware of the possibility of crises. Encouraging the new principal to develop sound time-management skills should be a priority of any mentor program.

Successful principals have developed time-management practices that have helped them survive. As a mentor, the experienced principal can guide and direct the beginning principal through a series of thought-provoking questions and suggestions to help become organized, and the new principal's stress level will be lessened. Time-management suggestions that mentors can review with the mentees might include any of the following:

1. *Tracking.* Have a method of keeping track of your tasks and schedules. You might use a pocket calendar, electronic notebook, PC, laptop, or plan book. Develop a method that works best for you.

2. *Reminders.* Keep a note pad, electronic notebook, or laptop with you to jot down reminders, thoughts, or ideas. Days can be hectic. Leaving things to memory may lead to problems.

3. *Commitments.* Enter scheduled dates and appointments when you become aware of them. District, cluster, level, staff, and committee meetings; professional development sessions; or mentor contacts may be regularly scheduled. Be sure your secretary knows you have commitments on those dates and times.

4. *School Schedules.* Establish a school calendar that will commit you to a routine for staff meetings, classroom observations, committee meetings, student progress reviews, parent meetings, appointments, and other planned activities. Be sure to include fire, disaster, and lock-down drills on this calendar. Making this calendar accessible to the appropriate staff and community leaders will be beneficial for their time management as well.

5. *Personal.* Include in your calendar a block of time for self-assessment and daily strategy and planning. (Remember to take care of yourself and your family.)

6. *Prioritizing.* Research indicates most people will accomplish the first three, four, or five items on a list of priorities. Make prioritized listings. Establish tentative completion dates for each item, i.e., reports, newsletters, supply orders, drills, classroom observations, evaluations. Enter those tentative dates on your calendar, computer, or electronic device in the order of importance. Nonurgent items can be worked on gradually in unscheduled time slots. Be conscious of deadlines.

7. *Procrastination.* Don't procrastinate! If you are a procrastinator, you must work hard to change. Procrastination is the worst enemy of time management. When tasks are on your priority list, complete them in a timely manner.

8. *Communication.* Other than important or emergency calls, which should be dealt with immediately, schedule a time to return phone messages and e-mails. Make every effort to respond to all messages within twenty-four hours. It's just good public relations!

9. *Paper Pushing.* Have your secretary sort mail grouped into two categories, "IMPORTANT" and "OTHER." Much of the "OTHER" will be junk mail that can be tossed or held for review later.

10. *Availability.* Be available and be visible. Be sure staff, parents, and students can communicate with you. Encourage staff and parents to make appointments when a block of time is needed to address their nonemergency concerns or issues. Many small issues can be dealt with on the go.

11. *Be Organized.* Have a place for everything and everything in its place. Organize your desk, files, and office so you know where everything is and can retrieve it quickly. Work with your secretary or a school volunteer to get organized.

12. *Delegate.* Get to know your staff and the students' parents. Delegate or empower committees or dependable individuals to work with some issues or suggest ideas for you. Remain informed about the progress of decisions and ideas that individuals recommend. This process will help with your time management while involving others.

> You cannot control time. You can only control what you do with it.
>
> —CJW

## THE IMPORTANCE OF STRONG INSTRUCTIONAL LEADERSHIP

Instructional leadership can be an enormous challenge for a new administrator, particularly in a school that has been identified as failing to meet adequate yearly progress, or a school that has been dealing with major conflicts. "Central office administrators and local school board members are much less tolerant of errors and poor performance than ever before" (Daresh, 2006a, p. 6). Attempting to implement major change before the new principal is established as a positive influence may be a mistake. Being an overzealous leader can be detrimental to a total program, but especially to the curriculum development process within that program. "A well-meaning and talented principal initiates curriculum reform, the teachers come on board because they have no choice, and the principal micromanages the effort. Implicitly he says: We're going to move forward, whether you like it or not. . . . As teachers begin to close their doors, morale and innovation decline along with communication" (Senge, Cambron-McCabe, Lucas, Smith, Dutton, & Kleiner, 2000, p. 92). This approach has little to do with becoming an instructional leader. A beginning principal with an overzealous leadership style should be advised by the mentor to step back and develop a positive school culture and to avoid embarking on a collision course with their teachers, as described above. A mentor may work with the mentee to analyze approaches for effective instructional leadership and help establish a vision for instructional challenges.

Increasing expectations by others and the need to become established in a new role adds additional stress. "The problem, of course, is that of moving too fast as a new leader has serious drawbacks. Change might occur, but the cost to the new person might be more than is reasonable as health begins to fail, personal relationships suffer, and followers get caught up in a hectic pace that cannot be maintained for very long" (Daresh, 2006b, p. 147). A mentor can be an invaluable resource in providing guidance and advice on how to pace oneself. A mentor's advice must be to move carefully in making major changes. Sharing strategies and helping the new administrator work through challenges can help alleviate some anxiety and stress.

The new principal can set the tone for review or change in the curriculum as well as in other areas. Recommendations must be justified with research, data, or rationale. The mentor may help review the school's vision for growth. Once the vision is determined, planning, training, and implementation can begin.

## DEMOGRAPHIC DATA FOR INSTRUCTIONAL IMPLEMENTATION

A schoolwide vision is paramount to effective instructional leadership. Mistakes are often made by creating the expectation that change must occur immediately. A new principal should have a good understanding of the school's demographics before a productive vision can be implemented. School demographics will play a significant role in the timing and implementation of change.

Mentors can be supportive by asking thought-provoking questions to distinguish perception from fact. At the onset of a new principal's appointment, the mentor and mentee should find time to review the concerns the mentee or the district might have about the curriculum, expectations, and goals. To minimize meeting time, the mentor might suggest the mentee prepare a list of issues and concerns that he or she perceives as potential conflicts, as expressed by key staff members, community leaders, or students. Remember, too, that district administrations and previous school administrators may have helpful information.

Usually, a comprehensive school assessment should be completed before major changes occur. With input from all sectors of the school community, a vision can move forward with positive outcomes. Many needs and directions can be identified through the use of demographic data. Unless essential or specifically directed, it may not be advisable to attempt to change too many things immediately after the new leader is appointed.

Beginning principals must prioritize their concerns based on school needs. The mentor may be able to assist by helping the mentee select one or two important issues, and then helping the mentee focus on a plan of action. The mentee must involve the staff, community, and students (when age appropriate) in this process and begin developing the concept of working together for the common good of the students. This approach can invoke a feeling of ownership and commitment to the overall school vision.

Following are some suggested questions that the mentor and mentee might pursue:

- What is the socioeconomic make-up of the student population?
- What are the demographics of the community?
- Does the school community have safety issues?
- What does the history of student test data reflect?
- What is vested in the existing curriculum?
- How do you quickly identify the strengths and weakness in the curriculum?
- What are the demographics of the staff?
- Can you identify the leaders on your staff? The dissenters?
- Are those leaders supportive of your appointment?
- Can you identify teachers who are not performing up to expectations?
- Is the staff a cohesive team?
- What condition is the school in (buildings, grounds, and maintenance)?
- Is it attractive in appearance? Does it evoke a sense of pride?
- Do you know your community leaders? Are they supportive of your appointment to *their* school?
- Is the political structure of the community understood?

A supportive mentor program should be mindful of the issues involved in change and encourage the mentee to approach change with wisdom and purpose. "Although it is certainly true that strong leadership from the principal can be a powerful force toward school reform, the notion that an individual can effect change by sheer will and personality is simply not supported by research. In fact, the evidence supports the assertion that a substantive change initiative must be supported both by administrators and by teachers" (Marzano, 2003, p. 174). In these days of *No Child Left Behind*, we need to understand that instruction is the number one priority and that adequate time for teacher involvement must be allotted to ensure positive outcomes for the students.

## THE EVALUATION PROCESS

Teacher evaluation is a critical part of the instructional process; it is the responsibility of the school administrator. The principal must schedule classroom observations and meet with every staff member to plan, develop, discuss, review, and approve professional development plans. Additional time may be required for any staff member who is on an improvement plan or on formal evaluation. It takes a great deal of time to schedule all the meetings that comply with the evaluation procedures alone. Often this evaluation process is regulated by school policy and negotiated agreements. The mentor can walk through the evaluation procedures with the mentee if the latter is not comfortable with the process.

## SCENARIO: RECIPROCAL MENTORING

Aubrey has nine years of experience as a middle school principal. She works in a community with a population of about sixty thousand. The school district has two high schools, four middle schools, and eighteen elementary schools. Jackie is a beginning principal at another middle school. The school district implemented a mentor program about three years ago. Jackie and Aubrey have known each other both professionally and socially for several years, so everyone felt comfortable when Aubrey agreed to be Jackie's mentor. Although Aubrey has not had any formal mentor training, she did purchase and read some books on mentoring and developed a knowledge base about the process. Aubrey and Jackie have been meeting and communicating on a regular basis. Jackie feels confident about the support she is receiving and does not hesitate to contact Aubrey when she has questions or concerns. Because of *No Child Left Behind* mandates and accountability, the school district decided to implement a computerized student data-tracking program. Aubrey and Jackie spent a great deal of time planning strategy for program implementation.

In the beginning of program implementation, the district required all administrators to participate in training sessions that focused on purpose, utilization of funds, and strategies for effective data tracking. This was a year-long process that was designed to be in place for the coming year. As the year progressed, Aubrey began to wonder who was mentoring whom. It became a team approach with both contributing to the development of their program, and truly became a reciprocal approach to mentoring. Although the close relationship has continued, both Jackie and Aubrey still argue about whether the mentee or the mentor received the most benefit from the experience.

### Scenario Conclusions

Mentors have often conveyed the feeling that they receive a reciprocal benefit from the mentoring experience. They have reflected this feeling in annual end-of-year ESP program surveys. A summarization of the annual survey has been shared with the school administrators at the end of each year. It is also published in the annual revised ESP handbooks. Daresh and Zachary also support the concept of reciprocal mentoring. "Mentoring involves the creation and maintenance of a mutually enhancing relationship in which both the mentor and the protégé can attain goals that are related to both personal development and career enhancement" (Daresh, 2001, p. 75). In her writings, Zachary refers to the process as "Reverse Mentoring" (2005, p. 194).

1. Mentors sense a feeling of enthusiasm that helps them become rejuvenated.

2. Mentees provide fresh ideas and approaches to current issues.

3. Mentors reevaluate practices.

4. Mentors revisit issues that have not surfaced recently. As one principal puts it, "It forced me to bone up on several aspects of my job that I had not thought about for years."

5. Mentoring provides the opportunity for sharing, problem solving, and venting.

6. The process gives a mentor satisfaction that he or she has gained professional respect.

## KEY POINTS

1. In the twelve years of the Albuquerque Extra Support for Principals mentor program, the three most frequently mentioned areas of concern for beginning principals were curriculum, time management, and budget. It is critical for any program planner or director to be respectful of a principal's time. This is even more true for the time of the beginning principal. Keep in mind that the new principal has to hit the ground running to address all the issues any principal must deal with on a day-to-day basis, and that the issues must be resolved with a certain degree of inexperience. Unless the new principal has already worked in the school as a teacher or assistant principal, a new principal must confront several things that an experienced principal does automatically, such as knowing staff names and their responsibilities at the school. Those are basics; it grows from there.

2. New principals must learn very quickly the demographics of the school, including school operations, staff strengths and weaknesses, curriculum, students, parents, and community.

3. Adding a simple mentoring system is a plus, but adding complex district mandates can create another level of frustration. It is very important to know district operational procedures and board policies. The process for ensuring that new principals are familiar with those procedures and policies can best be addressed through district planning and training initiatives.

4. Mentoring and training can come together to provide a total support system for the enthusiastic beginner. Experienced principals are an excellent resource for training, but their expertise should be utilized with thought and purpose. A mentor may serve a more useful purpose by reinforcing or clarifying the district's training and procedures.

5. Being an effective leader takes courage, tenacity, knowledge, and people skills.

6. It is easy to get caught up in day-to-day issues while neglecting the role of instructional leader. Assessing need and direction are ongoing tasks that must involve others.

7. Time is always a concern.

## RECOMMENDED READINGS

Daresh, J. C. (2006a). *Leading and supervising instruction,* Thousand Oaks, CA: Corwin Press.

Daresh, J. C. (2006b). *Beginning the principalship: A practical guide for new school leaders* (2nd ed.). Thousand Oaks, CA: Corwin Press.

Marzano, Robert J. (2003). *What works in schools: Translating research into action.* Alexandria, VA: Association for Supervision and Curriculum Development.

Senge, P., Cambron-McCabe, N., Lucas, T., Smith, B., Dutton, J., & Kleiner, A. (2000). *Schools that learn: A fifth discipline resource.* New York: Doubleday Publishing.

# Caution, Pitfalls Ahead!

# 10

Some have raised concerns about the average longevity of principals' careers and of mentoring programs. In response, we have reviewed mentoring program practices to create an awareness of potential pitfalls in a program's process. By identifying areas of concern, we hope to avoid situations that would have a negative impact on a mentor program and help alleviate some of the concerns. The following observations are not meant as criticisms, but rather as observations and findings based on the principles of cause and effect.

## IT'S ABOUT TIME

Experienced principals are protective of their time, as reflected in Dr. John Daresh's book, *Beginning the Principalship*, "[M]any principals speak jokingly about '8-day work weeks and 25-hour days'" (2006b, p. ix). When new programs, such as a mentoring program, are inserted into an already busy routine, principals may become cautious, skeptical, and even defensive. That does not imply lack of support, but initial support can quickly waver if principals fail to see positive results from their efforts. Add to the cadre of experienced administrators the new principal who has all the responsibilities of the experienced principal in addition to the added challenges of learning the demographics of a new school, staff, curriculum, inherited issues, or issues created by the change in leadership. The neophyte principal definitely has more to contend with and may not have developed a knowledge base to address some issues. If a new principal is offered support from a mentor program, he or she truly wants it to be support rather than a layer of administrative bureaucracy. Chapter 9, "Finding Time to Become an Instructional Leader," provides attention to the issue of time management and to the ways the mentor's guidance can help establish an effective routine for the mentee.

## THE FUNDING DILEMMA

Grants and fellowships for mentor programs are often developed for a period with the intent of establishing a district-funded program, and therein lies the dilemma. The program is implemented with strong financial backing and moves forward with all the descriptors prescribed for the program. When grant funding stops at the end of the grant period, the initiative must be absorbed by the program or the district or new proposals for additional grants must be written. Most initiatives require larger sums of money in the beginning stages of program development. In some cases, total program cost can exceed millions of dollars during the life of the grant. Replacing grant funds could be draining on a school district's budget and the program may begin to falter. In some cases, a district may decide to pull committed funds to address other district initiatives or concerns, leaving the program financially strapped. Dr. Lois Zachary (2005) observes, "The biggest and most difficult obstacle is honoring a financial commitment once it has been made, particularly in an already economically challenged market. . . . If the corporate bottom line is affected, executive leadership is often tempted to let go of the line item" (pp. 62–63).

It is important to look beyond the original funding source and envision how the program can be sustained after resources are depleted or withdrawn. Is there a long-range program? If grants are utilized, can the district continue to provide the same level of support after the grant funds are depleted? Grants provide additional resources, but the program foundation should be established within district means. Otherwise, the option is to depend on additional grants or allow the program to lapse. Approaching program development with this awareness can minimize the funding crisis in later years. In Chapter 2, "The Beginning of a Mentor Program," a simplistic approach to funding is covered in more detail. If funding is a major issue in the planning stages of a program, it can become a bigger issue later when the program is operational.

## PLAN, PLAN, PLAN

School districts develop ways to improve district programs and instruction. Focus may even be on the principalship as the instrument for change. Implementation of change may involve additional training and time commitments. Since districts do not have unlimited resources, personnel look for options and often turn to state, federal, or other monetary sources for funding innovative programs. Grants may come with accountability requirements such as external auditors, unusual documentation, and massive amounts of paperwork. This process takes time, which may have a negative impact on the people and district involved. Programs might be dropped, curtailed, or labeled unsuccessful.

Grants remain great resources for funding and should be pursued when grant funds are available. Grants are sometimes written specifically for mentor programs, while others may be written to include a mentor program as part of the total program. Because of the massive accountability requirements, much of the documentation for the grant falls on the mentor and mentee, which creates situations that subtract time from the school. Mentoring programs and funding sources should be considered only after a great deal of thought, analysis, and planning. Grant implementation, documentation, and evaluation demands can lead to major issues for staff. The director or coordinator of the program appears to be the most vulnerable to these demands. When change in school leadership occurs, the program focus often changes, or the program dissolves into an ineffective process. Not only does the program often suffer, but any investment of time and money is often wasted.

## DO NOT TAKE STRESS AND BURNOUT LIGHTLY

The terms "stress" and "burnout" are often used together, but they are different events. **Stress** is brought on by worrying about things that are going to happen, by events that could happen, or by events that might never happen. **Burnout** is a feeling of hopelessness and despair that can lead to a strong desire to extricate oneself from the situation. One important justification for a mentor program is to support new principals through a possibly stressful first-year adjustment—appropriate support from a mentor alleviates much of that stress.

Attempting to minimize stress for the beginning principal is a major focus of the safe, simple, and supportive concept. Several of the suggested reading materials reference stress as an occupational hazard of a principalship. Stress should not be taken lightly. It can impact mental and physical health and lead to withdrawal or capitulation. The district must be sensitive to the extra demands placed on a neophyte and make every attempt to provide a support system that will help the beginning principal progress through the rigors of transition into the role of a successful principal.

Minimizing additional expectations of a mentor program is a first step in creating success for the program and for the new principal. The safe, simple, and supportive philosophy does not minimize district expectations, but it can help the mentee satisfy those expectations. A rule of thumb is that if the mentor program is creating additional hardship for a principal it is not serving its intended purpose.

Identifying the symptoms and causes of stress and burnout is a positive step toward addressing the issue. The following information was obtained and summarized from two articles at the website Helpguide.org: "Stress: Signs and Symptoms, and Causes and Effects" and "Burnout Signs, Symptoms, and Prevention."

How one copes with an event is sometimes more of an issue than is the event itself. Stress levels will differ among individuals coping with the same event. When extreme physical or mental stress occurs, the body reacts through digestive disorders, tension or hypertension, headaches, aches and pains, sleep disorders, weight issues, immune deficiency disorders, other symptoms, or a combination of any of the above. Mental state can be affected by memory loss, poor concentration, weak decision-making skills, difficulty staying on task, or poor judgment. More detailed listings can be located from the website cited.

Stress appears to be more quickly identifiable than burnout and usually precedes burnout. Burnout symptoms are usually emotional rather than physical. Symptoms such as feelings of powerlessness, hopelessness, of being a failure, of being emotionally drained, or that one is not valued as an individual or as a contributor are some identifiers of burnout. By the time symptoms of burnout are identified, it is often too late. If the situational stress can be minimized, however, there is hope for recovery from burnout.

**Exhibit 10A**  Ways to Prevent Job Burnout

---

- Develop an effective time-management routine. (Refer to Chapter 9, "Finding Time to Become an Instructional Leader.")
- Seek collaboration.
- Clarify your job description.
- Request a transfer.
- Ask for new duties.
- Look for a new job.
- Make a career change.
- Get career advice.

---

*Source:* http://www.helpguide.org/mental/burnout_signs_symptoms.htm.

Although not part of an individual's suggested preventive measures, it would be incumbent on the supervisors to look for and provide ample opportunities for praise and recognition to those dedicated to their roles. If a supervisor can appropriately praise and encourage those who are struggling, positives may follow. If growth and improvement are established goals, sincere praise and recognition can be valuable assets in defusing stress and burnout.

Comparisons are made between the symptoms of stress and burnout in the article "Stress and Burnout in the Clergy," by Dr. Arch Hart. Dr. Hart's differentiations between stress and burnout are found in Exhibit 10B.

**Exhibit 10B** Dr. Arch Hart's Differentiations Between Stress and Burnout

| Stress | Burnout |
|---|---|
| . . . is characterized by overengagement. | . . . is characterized by disengagement. |
| . . . causes overreactive emotions. | . . . blunts emotions. |
| . . . produces urgency and hyperactivity. | . . . produces helplessness and hopelessness. |
| . . . exhausts physical energy. | . . . exhausts motivation, drive, and hope. |
| . . . leads to anxiety disorders. | . . . leads to paranoia and detachment. |
| . . . causes disintegration. | . . . causes demoralization. |
| . . . does physical damage primarily. | . . . does emotional damage primarily. |
| . . . may cause premature death. | . . . may cause premature death. |

*Source:* http://www.helpguide.org/mental/burnout_signs_symptoms.htm.

Although the following scenario is fictional, it is based on factual observations while I served as coordinator, advisor, and consultant to principal mentor programs.

## SCENARIO: A HEAVY LOAD

As Pam began working in her new position of project coordinator for the entire school district, she came in contact with the district principals on a regular basis. It became evident that newer principals needed additional support. Her research led to a focus on mentoring programs for principals. She surveyed the district principals. The survey results were overwhelmingly in support of such a program. She researched grant proposal writing. After she felt comfortable with the process, she identified a three-year grant valued at approximately $750,000 and began writing a proposal.

Based on research and best practices, Pam began to think and write about the many different ways she could support her new principals. She developed a budget that included the following line items:

- consultant fees
- an external auditor (which was required by the grantor)
- training for mentors and mentees
- in-service and institute opportunities with prominent guest speakers
- travel expenses for speakers, consultants, staff, and principals
- supplies
- equipment
- printed materials
- mileage for local travel
- salary compensation for project coordinator and program coordinator
- compensation for mentors

She developed job descriptions and program goals, purposes, guidelines, timelines, vision statement, mission statement, a program implementation process, and a tracking and evaluation component.

An external auditor and other staff were employed, and an advisory committee was established, composed of principals from all three instructional levels plus a representative from the district alternative programs. Procedures and guidelines were developed to comply with grant expectations. Surveys and questionnaires were developed to address grant compliance issues, including timelines, surveys, evaluation forms, and anecdotal record forms, which were reproduced and placed in binders for all participants. Potential mentors were identified, mentor-mentee pairings were made, and training sessions ensued.

A year later, Pam was beginning to feel some frustration because of the level of responsibility she had for managing the grant: she had to compile the principals' information, attend the many meetings and training sessions, and address noncompliance issues. The superintendent wanted to add additional training sessions for new principals. Getting the data from principals was becoming time consuming for Pam.

Pam was spending evenings at her office organizing meetings, planning workshops, collecting data, communicating with principals, and writing program justifications for the district and auditors, in addition to performing her regular project coordinator responsibilities. She was also beginning to hear concerns from both mentors and mentees about being pulled out of their schools too often. Some were even choosing not to attend some of the scheduled meetings, training sessions, or all-day institutes because of other school commitments.

During the second year of the program, Pam resigned. After Pam's departure, another person was assigned the district project manager coordinator position. The massive demands of the program became overwhelming for the new person. Because more and more grant guidelines were gradually not being met, the grant funds were lost for the third year. Some experienced principals continued to support the new appointees without much direction from the district because of their own professionalism.

## Scenario Conclusions

Foundations generously give out millions of dollars each year with goals to support worthwhile endeavors. In this case, though, the way the grant was structured seemed to be part of the problem.

1. Accountability was required both for program development and for money spent.

2. Documentation was required to support the goals and objectives of the grant.

3. Collecting data was time consuming.

4. Principals were called on frequently to respond to reports, surveys, and questionnaires after attending institutes.

5. Mentees and mentors had to keep anecdotal records on all contacts, which was an additional burden with little direct benefit to the principals.

6. Participants questioned the benefits of the time and paperwork required by the mentoring process.

7. Because of increased levels of demands and stress, mentors were being forced to choose between filling out forms and attending meetings, or meeting the needs of their own schools.

8. Pam did not have experience as a principal. She developed a program to obtain a large grant without sufficient knowledge and background of the principalship. The demands and activities became overwhelming to her—physically and mentally—as well as to the participants in their schools. Most principals are willing to support mentoring as long as it does not become time consuming and interfere with their responsibilities at their own schools.

## SUPERINTENDENTS AND
## UPPER-LEVEL ADMINISTRATION

Upper-level administrators can have a strong impact on the development of a principal mentor program. No matter what the funding source might be, when upper-level administrators accept the basic concept that mentoring should be a safe support system for new principals, a successful mentoring program can be developed. When superintendents or upper-level administrators agree to support a program and then begin using it as a catchall for solutions to district problems, the program tends to lose its effectiveness. Hopefully, a superintendent will be able to channel those district issues and concerns through other personnel and departments, leaving the mentoring concept intact. When this does not occur, the mentor program will become another layer of district mandates and will do little to promote the professional development of a principal in transition. On occasion, good people can make wrong decisions, and the impact can reach far beyond the intended outcome. Sometimes when upper-level administrators act without considering the consequences, there can be an unintended effect on a program. The following scenario is an example of how persons of authority can impact an outcome without realizing the consequences of their decisions.

## SCENARIO: SOLVE THE PROBLEM

Maralee has been coordinating her school district's principal mentor program for two years. In early September, Maralee's superintendent, José, called her and asked if she could help in assigning a mentor to one of the district principals who had been in the same school for several years. José felt this principal was having difficulty and could benefit from having a mentor. However, Maralee explained to the superintendent that other means of support should be considered instead of the mentoring program. She gave several reasons. First, if this principal is having problems, future evaluations would be based on the areas in question. Maralee reminded José that the mentor program was designed to be a safe relationship between the mentee and mentor, and that the mentor should not be placed in the position of evaluating or even reporting back to an evaluator. She also pointed out that assigning a mentor to a troubled principal would set a precedent for the mentor program that could leave the impression that the program was for principals in need of corrective intervention. Principals would not want to be associated with a stigmatized program. The superintendent concurred and expressed appreciation for Maralee's insight.

## Scenario Conclusions

José was looking for an easy way to resolve a problem without considering the impact or the outcome. Upper-level administrators and principals often look at situations from different perspectives. The fact that many superintendents have moved through the principal ranks may have little or no bearing on their decisions. A superintendent's perspective of the total picture becomes much broader; this distance can become greater over time.

### KEY POINTS

It is disturbing to see a mentor program fail. To determine the cause of the failure, we must first look at the management of the program, program goals, objectives, and whether or not design procedures were followed. A committee review might include staffing, budgeting, and unexpected issues to determine where the problems might lie. Reassessment and reorganization may be required. Problems and issues might be avoided by reviewing the three basic principles: safe, simple, and supportive.

1. *Is the program safe?* Do the mentees have a trusting relationship with their mentors? Are the mentors nonjudgmental? Is there an open positive relationship between mentor and mentee? Are mentors providing that safe environment where those very simple questions might be asked? Several authors write about this issue in greater detail: Villani (2006); Daresh (2001); Zachary (2000); and Bloom, Castagna, Moir, and Warren (2005).

2. *Is the program simple?* Keeping the program simple is tied directly to the program's use of time. Is the program making effective use of time for both the mentor and mentee? Is the program providing the opportunity for a new principal to access the knowledge, advice, and expertise of an experienced principal (mentor) in a nonthreatening and timely fashion? Are principals being pulled from their schools too often or asked too frequently to be involved in time-consuming tasks? Are activities and data gathering beneficial to the mentoring process or to the justification of the program? Do mentors and other participants believe their time is being utilized effectively in support of the mentee?

3. *Is the program supportive?* Is the mentor-mentee relationship one that conveys trust, respect, and confidence? Has a supportive and comfortable communication plan been developed? Zachary (2005) stresses the importance of communication in recent writings (pp. 137–161).

*(Continued)*

(Continued)

Weakness in any of these three areas could hamper success of the growth of the mentor-mentee program. Safety and simplicity are critical. Supportive mentors encourage positive growth and reinforcement to ensure success.

1. It is not uncommon for a program director or coordinator to find the mentor pool diminishing. Experienced principals who are mentors will be the first to pull back if they feel their own school is beginning to suffer because their time is not being utilized effectively. New principals who are mentees may be reluctant to respond in that manner. As new principals, they are aware of the district's expectation and mandates for beginning principals and do not want to appear weak or ineffective.

2. Stress or burnout: both can have serious consequences if not recognized and addressed in a timely manner. It is important to realize how stressful the first year of a principalship can be. Adding burdens and tasks not directly related to their school will add to the level of stress. Some beginning principals decide to return to the classroom because they have been overwhelmed by some of the demands of their mentor-mentee induction program.

3. The funding dilemma needs analysis. Establish the true purpose for support: If the purpose is to provide endless opportunities for professional development, in-service, institutes, research, and data collecting, abundant financial resources will be needed. If the program intent is to provide a mentor support system that will help guide the mentee through the first year's growth and challenges, minimal financial support will be needed. A reasonable number of professional development and in-service opportunities can be provided at nominal cost, and often can be funded through support from the business community.

4. Real value for the mentee comes from the one-on-one support offered in a successful mentoring environment.

   In our work around the country, we have asked hundreds of principals how they acquired the many skills and broad knowledge essential to their jobs in the teaching role, in pre-service and in-service programs, through life experiences, or on the job? They report that their most important learning takes place on the job—and note that pre-service and in-service programs are among the least significant sources of preparation for the principalship. This is supported by a recent survey conducted by Public Agenda, in which 80 percent of superintendents and 69 percent of principals reported that graduate programs do not meet the needs of today's school leaders. (Bloom et al., 2005, p. 11)

What better way to support new principals than to have experienced principals available to support and direct their learning experiences?

5. There are predictors that can help determine the success or ineffectiveness of a mentor program. A sampling of some of the more obvious ones are found in Exhibit 10C.

**Exhibit 10C** Predictors of a Mentor Program's Success or Failure

| Positive | Negative |
| --- | --- |
| Limited meetings with purpose | Excessive meetings |
| Minimal documentation | Excessive documentation |
| Superintendents that understand process | Lack of understanding from superintendents |
| District support | Lack of commitment from the district |
| Effective time-management skills | Poor time-management skills |
| Strong mentor commitment | Lack of mentor commitment |
| Purposeful communication | Inability to communicate |
| Respect of principals' time | Lack of consideration of principals' time |
| Support from district's principals | Lack of support from district's principals |
| Using qualified principals as mentors | Using unqualified principals as mentors |
| Providing basic mentor training | Not providing mentor training |
| Low-stress programming | Creating stress and burnout in program |
| Activities that promote growth | Activities with little purpose for principals |
| Adequate program funding | Loss of program funds |

*Source:* Carl J. Weingartner

# RECOMMENDED READINGS

Helpguide.org. "Stress: Signs and symptoms, and causes and effects." http://www.helpguide.org/mental/stress_signs.htm.

Helpguide.org. "Burnout signs, symptoms, and prevention." http://www.helpguide.org/mental/burnout_signs_symptoms.htm.

# Reflections     **11**

According to the National Association of Elementary School Principals, the principalship in this country is in crisis. As a nation, we must give serious consideration to more effective recruiting and retaining of principals. Larger districts may be faced with the loss of vast numbers of principals or a depleted principal applicant pool. Daresh (2006b) writes, "It is not uncommon to hear of situations where large school districts are facing the need to hire 20% or more new principals each year for the foreseeable future" (p. ix). Based on national and state administrators associations and educational agencies surveys, Daresh goes on to indicate, "within the next few years more than half of the principals in the United States (and in many other countries around the world) will be able to retire and leave the school principalship if they desire" (p. 2). Today, some large school districts across the nation are seeing many veteran principals retiring earlier than previously planned. These same districts have a high percentage of principals with five or fewer years of experience. Districts must reach beyond their area or region to advertise principal openings. Use of the Internet is one relatively new approach in the search for qualified applicants. Many districts resort to filling the positions with acting principals or with individuals willing to request provisional administrative licensure or certification, which implies additional course work and responsibilities in addition to an already demanding routine.

Time, stress, or burnout continue to be factors that can lead to frustration and even the professional demise of almost any leader, if not dealt with in a proactive way. Mentors and coordinators must be constantly aware that time represents an important factor; the time spent with a beginning principal must be productive and encouraging. The mentor needs to be aware that, because of the mentee's inexperience, time initially will be a major concern. Tasks or issues that are initially challenges for the beginning principal will eventually become simple; however, once knowledge and experience are gained, these tasks and issues should invoke automatic responses with little thought or deliberation.

Program data must be gathered to establish program creditability, but discretionary judgment must be used in deciding how much time is spent gathering data and filling out forms. The mentor program should use data-gathering tools sparingly if the purpose is to effectively support a new principal during that transformational year. According to Susan Villani's research, some states and school districts are beginning actually to mandate principal mentoring programs. In her research, she has identified several states and local districts that have mandated mentor programs for beginning principals (Villani, 2006, pp. 79–227). Some states and school districts provide some program funding, i.e., state funds, district funds, private funds, or grants. Some of these programs may require massive amounts of documentation in order to comply with funding requirements. These requirements could have a direct impact on the beginning principal performance and morale if they become overwhelming and burdensome.

One must realize that beginning principals often enter the position both excited and anxious about the challenges to come. They may not feel comfortable in expressing frustrations because they are afraid they might be perceived as ineffective. New principals may be coping with issues and mandates in a foreign, questioning, or even hostile environment. Mentoring programs are often established with good intentions of support, but the reality is sometimes different. Some districts use the mentor position as a way to oversee the neophyte's performance. Most would agree that a new principal must be held accountable and that the mentoring process should not carry the burden of accountability. The mentor plays an important role in the total process as an advisor to the mentee. This protects the security and confidentiality of the mentor-mentee relationship. The primary objective of a mentor program must be to help the mentee to develop and to become an effective leader.

*No Child Left Behind* (NCLB) has caused education to undergo a transformation. Those who are less able to adapt are going to have difficulty remaining in a leadership position. Since January 2002, the climate of standards, laws, testing, guidelines, and accountability has changed the delivery of instruction. Strategies and teaching methods have had to be revisited or revised, curricula are being overhauled, and mandates and consequences have been developed for schools. Striving to meet state and national standards has become a primary focus for many districts and schools. Preparing for mandated tests takes a disproportional amount of instructional time. It has become evident through observation and research that NCLB has caused educational training for teachers and principals to become more rigorous. Conversely, though, salaries have not kept pace with these added demands. Principals are subjected to more pressure than ever before. Their job security has become unstable in many situations. Some administrators have been transferred or demoted, while others have been terminated because they have been unable to achieve NCLB Adequate Yearly Progress (AYP) performance goals for their school. Adding the NCLB climate to the challenges and demands of schools creates situations in which educators may become disenchanted with the educational process.

Most educators come into the principalship enthusiastic, energetic, knowledgeable, and dedicated. They are not afraid to devote the time and energy it takes to do the job. As Daresh indicates, they would love to have twenty-five hours in a day. These are the same attributes corporate America is looking for when they recruit, and corporations have more to offer: higher salaries, more training, better fringe benefits, and bonus incentives that look very attractive to the educator. Often, the positive benefits of remaining in the classroom as a teacher may seem to outweigh any reasons for pursuing a principalship, which only seems to offer increased levels of stress and responsibility, longer contracts, and inequitable salaries. These are the main reasons why many administratively qualified educators are choosing not to leave the classroom for careers as principals. In some cases, first- and second-year principals are leaving the principalship for the same reasons.

A review of the research leaves little doubt that the principalship is a position that is becoming less attractive for many. According to the Institute for Educational Leadership IEL, 2000, "Eighty-six percent of the superintendents interviewed in 1998 discussed the difficulty in filling principalship openings in their districts" (Villani, 2006, p. 6). If school districts fail to find ways to attract and retain quality recruits, their principal pools may become depleted or the quality of prospective principals may decline. Active recruitment must be part of the process. Principal recruitment within the staff, educational incentives, attractive salaries, and an adequate support system can all be used to promote the principalship.

When designing a mentor program, be respectful of the time issue and work toward a safe, simple, and supportive plan that will encourage educators to pursue a career as a principal.

## RECOMMENDED READINGS

Daresh, J. C. (2006b). *Beginning the principalship: A practical guide for new school leaders* (2nd ed.). Thousand Oaks, CA: Corwin Press.

National Association of Elementary School Principals. (March 2001). The principalship in crisis. *Principal, 80*(4).

Villani, S. (2006). *Mentoring and induction programs that support new principals.* Thousand Oaks, CA: Corwin Press.

# References

Albuquerque Public Schools Leadership. (n.d.). http://www.apsleadership.com/.

Albuquerque Public Schools. http://ww2.aps.edu.

Barnett, B. G. (1987). *Instructional leadership concepts, issues and controversies: Using reflection as a professional growth activity.* Columbus, OH: Allyn & Bacon.

Bloom, G., Castagna, C., Moir, E., & Warren, B. (2005). *Blended coaching: Skills and strategies to support principal development.* Thousand Oaks, CA: Corwin Press.

Daresh, J. C. (2001). *Leaders helping leaders: A practical guide to administrative mentoring.* Thousand Oaks, CA: Corwin Press.

Daresh, J. C. (2006a). *Leading and supervising instruction.* Thousand Oaks, CA: Corwin Press.

Daresh, J. C. (2006b). *Beginning the principalship: A practical guide for new school leaders* (2nd Ed.). Thousand Oaks, CA: Corwin Press.

George Lucas Educational Foundation. (2002). Principles for mentoring principals. *Edutopia.* http://www.edutopia.org/principles-mentoring-principals

Guterman, J. (April/May 2007). Where have all the principals gone? The acute school-leader shortage. *Edutopia.* http://www.edutopia.org/where-have-all-principals-gone.

Helpguide.org. "Burnout signs, symptoms, and prevention." http://www.helpguide.org/mental/burnout_signs_symptoms.htm.

Helpguide.org. "Stress: Signs and symptoms, and causes and effects." http://www.helpguide.org/mental/stress_signs.htm.

Institute for Educational Leadership (IEL). (2000). *Leadership for student learning: Reinventing the principalship. School leadership for the 21st century initiative.* Washington, DC: Task Force on the Principalship.

Institute for Educational Leadership (IEL). (2005). "Preparing leaders for rural schools: Practice and policy considerations." IEL, Washington, DC. http://www.iel.org/pubs/ruralleaders.pdf.

Marzano, R. J. (2003). *What works in schools: Translating research into action.* Alexandria, VA: Association for Supervision and Curriculum Development.

Mission Expert. (n.d.). Creating effective mission and vision statements. http://www.mission-vision-ebook.com/.

Mission Expert. (n.d.). Example mission statement. http://www.missionexpert.com/information/mission-statement-examples.html.

National Association of Elementary School Principals. (March 2001). "The principalship in crisis." *Principal* 80(4).

Nightingale Conant. (n.d.). Example mission statement. http://www.nightingale
.com/mission_select.aspx

Schools in Albuquerque Public Schools. (n.d.). http://www.greatschools.net/
schools.page?district=4&state=NM.

Senge, P., Cambron-McCabe, N., Lucas, T., Smith, B., Dutton, J., & Kleiner, A. (2000).
*Schools that learn: A fifth discipline resource.* New York: Doubleday Publishing.

Villani, S. (2006). *Mentoring and induction programs that support new principals.*
Thousand Oaks, CA: Corwin Press.

Weingartner, C. J. (2001) "Albuquerque principals have ESP." *Principal: The
Principalship in Crisis, 80*(4), 40–42. National Association of Elementary
School Principals, Alexandria, VA.

Weingartner, C. J. (2002). "Principles for mentoring principals". *Edutopia.* http://www
.edutopia.org/principles-mentoring-principals

Weingartner, C. J. (2006). *Principals' mentorship program: Extra support for principals.* Albuquerque, NM: Albuquerque Public Schools.

Young, P., Sheets, J., & Knight, D. (2005). *Mentoring principals: Framework, agendas, tips. and case stories for mentors and mentees.* Thousand Oaks, CA: Corwin
Press.

Zachary, L. J. (2000). *The mentors' guide: Facilitating effective learning relationships.*
San Francisco: Jossey-Bass.

Zachary, L. J. (2005). *Creating a mentoring culture: The organizational guide.* San
Francisco: Jossey-Bass.

# Index

Accountability
 alternative assessments in, 49–54
 anecdotal reflections in, 52–54
 end-of-year evaluations and, 49, 50–51
   (exhibit)
 individual feedback and, 49
Acknowledgment and congratulations, 33
Administrators, 64, 92–93
Albuquerque Public School District
 birth of the mentor program in, 10
 demographics, 9, 40
 Extra Support for Principals (ESP)
   program, 1, 3, 17, 52–54, 55
   (exhibit), 56–58, 76
 mentoring coordinator, 10 (box),
   12–13, 20
 as a model for others, 69
 Principals Association, 10, 17
 program implementation, 25–32
 support for new principals, 22
Alternative assessments, 49–54
Anecdotal reflections, 52–54
Application, mentor, 43, 65 (exhibit)
Appreciation and recognition, 35–36, 37
Armstrong, Glenda, 52–53
Assessments
 alternative, 49–54
 ten-year program, 56–58
Availability and time, 78

Barnett, Bruce, 69
Beginning the Principalship, 85
Bloom, G., 6, 68
Budgeting and funding for mentor
   programs, 10–11, 42–43, 86, 89–91
Burnout, 87–89
Business partners, 37

Cambron-McCabe, N., 79
Castagna, C., 6, 68

Celebrations and social activities, 30–31,
   33–34
Charter schools, 39
Coaching
 concept, 69–70
 versus mentoring, 68–69
Commitments, time, 77
Communication, 29–30, 34–35, 71–72
 time and, 78
Compensation, principal, 4–5
Congratulations and acknowledgment, 33
Coordinators, mentor program, 12–13, 20
 compensation, 10 (box), 42
 conferring with mentors, 27–28, 44
 initial contact with new principals, 25
 initial meeting with mentees, 26–27
 job description, 18–19
Culminating activities, 31–32

Daresh, John C., 61, 71, 78, 79, 85,
   97, 99
Delegation, 78
Demographics
 Albuquerque Public School District,
   9, 40
 data for instructional implementation,
   79–81
Dutton, J., 79

Effective mentoring, 62–63
End-of-year evaluations, 49, 50–51
   (exhibit)
Enhancements, program
 appreciation as, 35–36, 37
 celebrations as, 30–31, 33–34
 communication, 29–30, 34–35
 congratulations as, 33
 morale and, 36
Espinosa, Peter, 10
Establishment of mentor pools, 63–66

Evaluations
    end-of-year, 49, 50–51 (exhibit)
    program, 54, 55 (exhibit)
    teacher, 81
Example Mission Statement, 16
Extra Support for Principals (ESP), 1, 3,
    11, 52–54, 55 (exhibit), 76
    mobility rates, 56–58
    as a model for other programs, 69
    program assessment, 56–58
    reverse mentoring and, 82

Feedback, individual, 49
Fellowships, 86
Funding for mentor programs, 10–11,
    42–43, 86, 89–91

George Lucas Educational Foundation, 66
Grants, 86–87, 89–91
Guidelines, program, 17–18
Guterman, J., 4

Hamilton, Debbie, 53
Handbook distribution, 29–30
Hart, Arch, 89
Hernandez-Alzaga, Manuel, 53

Implementation, program
    demographic data for, 79–81
    initial coordinator-mentee meeting in,
      26–27
    mentor-coordinator conference in,
      27–28
    mentor coordinator initial contact with
      principals in, 25
    planning session between mentor and
      mentee in, 29
    supportive activities and
      communications in, 29–32
Individual feedback, 49
Institute for Educational Leadership, 40, 99

Job descriptions, 18–20

Kleiner, A., 79

Leadership, instructional
    importance of strong, 78–79
    reciprocal mentoring and, 81–82
    time management and, 76–78
Level-to-level mentoring, 71
Lucas, T., 79
Luján, James, 54

Marzano, R. J., 81
Mentees. *See* Principals
Mentoring
    administrators and, 64, 92–93
    in the Albuquerque Public School
      District, 10–13
    as an art, 61
    celebrations and social activities,
      30–31, 33–34
    versus coaching, 68–69
    commitment, 4
    communication and, 29–30, 34–35,
      71–72
    concepts for effective, 62–63
    coordinators, 10 (box), 12–13, 18–19,
      20, 25–32
    culminating activities, 31–32
    development of, 10, 15
    funding and budgeting for, 10–11,
      42–43, 86, 89–91
    job descriptions, 18–20
    level-to-level, 71
    misconception about, 11 (box)
    people with gifts for, 61
    professional development, 31
    program guidelines, 17–18
    program process, 20–21
    reasons for, 3–5
    reciprocal, 81–82
    reflections on, 52–54, 97–99
    safe, simple and support concepts in, 4
    in small school districts, 45–46
    support for, 4, 21–22, 36–38, 70–71,
      80–81
    time, 5, 75, 76–78, 85
    vision and mission statements, 16–17
    *See also* Enhancements, program;
      Implementation, program
Mentoring and Induction Programs That
    Support New Principals, 58
Mentors
    applications, 43, 65 (exhibit)
    coaching and, 68–70
    communication with mentees, 71–72
    compensation, 11 (box), 36, 42
    coordinators conferring with,
      27–28, 44
    effective, 62–63
    end-of-year evaluations, 49, 51
      (exhibit)
    establishing a pool of, 63–66
    identification of, 43–44
    job description, 19–20

people gifted as, 61
planning sessions with mentees, 29
reflections of, 52–54
selected by committee, 64
suggestions for working with mentees,
    66–68
training, 30
wisdom, 72–73
Mission and vision statements, 16–17
Mission Expert: Creating Effective Mission
    and Vision Statements, 16
Mobility rates, 56–58
Moir, E., 6, 68
Morale factor, 36

National Association of Elementary
    School Principals, 4, 7, 97
National Association of Secondary School
    Principals, 7
Newsletters, bimonthly, 29–30
No Child Left Behind, 3, 5, 22, 40, 81, 98–99

Oman, Letha, 53–54
Organizations, professional, 6–7

Personal time, 77
Planning
    grant, 86–87
    session, mentor-mentee, 29
Pools, establishing mentor, 63–66
Principals
    anatomy of, 5–6
    compensation of, 4–5
    end-of-year evaluations, 49, 50
        (exhibit)
    first contact with coordinators, 25
    initial meeting with coordinator, 26–27
    planning sessions with mentors, 29
    professional organizations for, 6–7
    reasons for mentoring, 3–5
    reflections of, 52–54
    retention of, 4–5
    stress and, 5, 70–71, 87–91
    time required of, 5
    total support systems for, 21–22
Prioritizing time, 77
Process, program, 20–21
Procrastination, 77
Professional development, 31
Professional organizations, 6–7

Reciprocal mentoring, 81–82
Recognition and appreciation, 35–36, 37

Reflections, 97–99
    anecdotal, 52–54
Reminders, task, 77
Render, Mary, 54
Retention of principals, 4–5
Reverse mentoring, 82
Rural schools. *See* Small school districts

Safe environment for principals, 4, 70–71
Schedules, school, 77
Senge, P., 79
Simple mentoring processes, 4
Small school districts
    demographics, 39–40
    geographic isolation and technology
        use in, 44–45
    mentoring scenario, 45–46
    mentors in, 43–45
    organizing study committees for, 41
    purpose of study committees in,
        41–45
Smith, B., 79
Social activities and celebrations, 30–31,
    33–34
Stress and principals, 5, 70–71, 87–91
Study committees
    organizing, 41
    purpose of, 41–45, 64
Superintendents, 64, 92–93
Support for mentoring programs, 4,
    21–22, 36–38, 70–71, 80–81
Supportive activities and communications
    during mentoring, 29–32, 72–73
Surveys, 49, 50–51 (exhibit)

Technology and geographic issues,
    44–45
Ten-year program assessments, 56–58
Time
    challenges, 85
    management, 76–78
    required of principals and mentors,
        5, 75, 76
Tracking, task, 77
Training, mentor, 30

Villani, Susan, 5, 58, 61, 66, 98, 99
Vision and mission statements, 16–17

Warren, B., 6, 68
Weingartner, Carl J., 7–8, 52

Zachary, Lois, 29, 34, 68, 82, 86

**CORWIN
PRESS**

The Corwin Press logo—a raven striding across an open book—represents the union of courage and learning. Corwin Press is committed to improving education for all learners by publishing books and other professional development resources for those serving the field of PreK–12 education. By providing practical, hands-on materials, Corwin Press continues to carry out the promise of its motto: **"Helping Educators Do Their Work Better."**

NSDC's mission is to ensure success for all students by serving as the international network for those who improve schools and by advancing individual and organization development.

# PRINCIPAL
# MENTORING